Security for Telecommunications Networks

Advances in Information Security

Sushil Jajodia
Consulting Editor
Center for Secure Information Systems
George Mason University
Fairfax, VA 22030-4444
email: jajodia@gmu.edu

The goals of the Springer International Series on ADVANCES IN INFORMATION SECURITY are, one, to establish the state of the art of, and set the course for future research in information security and, two, to serve as a central reference source for advanced and timely topics in information security research and development. The scope of this series includes all aspects of computer and network security and related areas such as fault tolerance and software assurance.

ADVANCES IN INFORMATION SECURITY aims to publish thorough and cohesive overviews of specific topics in information security, as well as works that are larger in scope or that contain more detailed background information than can be accommodated in shorter survey articles. The series also serves as a forum for topics that may not have reached a level of maturity to warrant a comprehensive textbook treatment.

Researchers, as well as developers, are encouraged to contact Professor Sushil Jajodia with ideas for books under this series.

Additional titles in the series:

INSIDER ATTACK AND CYBER SECURITY: Beyond the Hacker edited by Salvatore Stolfo, Steven M. Bellovin, Angelos D. Keromytis, Sara Sinclaire, Sean W. Smith; ISBN: 978-0-387-77321-6

INTRUSION DETECTION SYSTEMS edited by Robert Di Pietro and Luigi V. Mancini; ISBN: 978-0-387-77265-3

VULNERABILITY ANALYSIS AND DEFENSE FOR THE INTERNET edited by Abhishek Singh; ISBN: 978-0-387-74389-9

BOTNET DETECTION: Countering the Largest Security Threat edited by Wenke Lee, Cliff Wang and David Dagon; ISBN: 978-0-387-68766-7

PRIVACY-RESPECTING INTRUSION DETECTION by Ulrich Flegel; ISBN: 978-0-387-68254-9

SYNCHRONIZING INTERNET PROTOCOL SECURITY (SIPSec) by Charles A. Shoniregun; ISBN: 978-0-387-32724-2

SECURE DATA MANAGEMENT IN DECENTRALIZED SYSTEMS edited by Ting Yu and Sushil Jajodia; ISBN: 978-0-387-27694-6

NETWORK SECURITY POLICIES AND PROCEDURES by Douglas W. Frye; ISBN: 0-387-30937-3

DATA WAREHOUSING AND DATA MINING TECHNIQUES FOR CYBER SECURITY by Anoop Singhal; ISBN: 978-0-387-26409-7

SECURE LOCALIZATION AND TIME SYNCHRONIZATION FOR WIRELESS SENSOR AND AD HOC NETWORKS edited by Radha Poovendran, Cliff Wang, and Sumit Roy; ISBN: 0-387-32721-5

PRESERVING PRIVACY IN ON-LINE ANALYTICAL PROCESSING (OLAP) by Lingyu Wang, Sushil Jajodia and Duminda Wijesekera; ISBN: 978-0-387-46273-8

SECURITY FOR WIRELESS SENSOR NETWORKS by Donggang Liu and Peng Ning; ISBN: 978-0-387-32723-5

MALWARE DETECTION edited by Somesh Jha, Cliff Wang, Mihai Christodorescu, Dawn Song, and Douglas Maughan; ISBN: 978-0-387-32720-4

Additional information about this series can be obtained from http://www.springer.com

Security for Telecommunications Networks

by

Patrick Traynor
Georgia Instutite of Technology, Atlanta, GA, USA

Patrick McDaniel
Thomas La Porta
Penn State University, University Park, PA, USA

 Springer

Authors
Patrick Traynor
Georgia Institute of Technology
College of Computing
Mail code 0765
Atlanta, GA 30332-0765
traynor@cc.gatech.edu

Patrick McDaniel
Penn State University
Dept. Computer Science & Engineering
360A IST Bldg.
University Park PA 16802
mcdaniel@cse.psu.edu

Thomas La Porta
Penn State University
Dept. Computer Science & Engineering
360B IST Bldg.
University Park PA 16802
tlp@cse.psu.edu

Series Editor
Sushil Jajodia
George Mason University
Center for Secure Information Systems
4400 University Drive
Fairfax VA 22030-4444, USA
jajodia@gmu.edu

ISBN: 978-1-4419-4438-2   e-ISBN: 978-0-387-72442-3

springer.com

For Mom, Dad, Tara and Sheila
–P. T.

For Megan, Sinclair, and Emerson
–P.M.

For Lisa, Abigail and Sophia
–T.L.

Contents

1 Introduction 1
   1.1 Telecommunications Networks 2
   1.2 Network Convergence and Security 3
   1.3 Outline of this Book 4
   1.4 Audience 5
   1.5 Other Sources of Information 6

Part I Network Architecture

2 Security 9
   2.1 Overview 9
      2.1.1 What is security? 9
      2.1.2 Basic Terminology 10
      2.1.3 Attacks 11
      2.1.4 Trust 11
   2.2 Services and Tools 12
      2.2.1 Cryptography 12
      2.2.2 Authentication and Authorization 15
      2.2.3 Certificates and PKI 16
   2.3 Network Security 16
      2.3.1 IPsec 16
      2.3.2 SSL/TLS 18
      2.3.3 Firewalls 19
      2.3.4 Intrusion and Anomaly Detection 20
   2.4 Summary 22

3 Cellular Architecture 23
   3.1 History of Cellular Telephony 24
   3.2 Cellular Voice Networks 26
      3.2.1 Voice Network Elements 26

3.2.2   Home Location Register 27
3.2.3   Mobile Switching Center/Visiting Location Register ... 29
3.2.4   Base Station Subsystem 29
3.3 Cellular Data Networks 30
3.3.1   Data Network Elements 30
3.3.2   Gateway GPRS Support Node 31
3.3.3   Serving GPRS Support Node 32
3.4 Signaling Network and Protocols 33
3.4.1   Common Channel Signaling Network 34
3.4.2   Message Transfer Part 34
3.4.3   Signaling Connection Control Part.................. 35
3.4.4   Transaction Capabilities Application Part 36
3.4.5   Mobile Application Part............................ 36
3.4.6   ISDN User Part 36
3.5 Wireless Network.. 36
3.5.1   Wireless Access Techniques 37
3.5.2   Frequency Issues 39
3.5.3   Voice Encoding 43
3.5.4   Summary of Procedures 45
3.6 Registration and Call Setup Procedures 46
3.7 Core Network Security 48
3.8 Air Interface Security 49
3.9 Summary... 51

Part II Vulnerability Analysis

4   Vulnerabilities in the Telephony 55
4.1 Weak Cryptographic Algorithms 55
4.2 Vulnerabilities in the Network Core 58
4.3 Wireless Eavesdropping 60
4.4 Jamming 61
4.5 User Tracking and Privacy............................... 62
4.6 Overload 62
4.7 Malware.. 63

5   Vulnerabilities in the Short Messaging Service (SMS)...... 65
5.1 History and Description 66
5.2 Delivering Messages 66
5.2.1   Submitting a Message.............................. 66
5.2.2   Routing a Message 67
5.2.3   Wireless Delivery................................. 68
5.3 Identifying System Bottlenecks 69
5.3.1   Queue Management 70
5.3.2   Message Injection 71

5.4   Efficient Device Targeting 72
     5.4.1   NPA/NXX 73
     5.4.2   Web Scraping 73
     5.4.3   Testing Phone "Liveness" 74
     5.4.4   Additional Collection Methods 75
5.5   Modeling Denial of Service 76
     5.5.1   Attacking Individuals 76
     5.5.2   Metropolitan Area Service 77
     5.5.3   Regional Service 81
5.6   Network Characterization 82
5.7   Attack Characterization 85
5.8   Current Solutions 87
5.9   Queue Management 89
     5.9.1   Weighted Fair Queuing 89
     5.9.2   Weighted Random Early Detection 92
     5.9.3   Summary 96
5.10 Resource Provisioning 96
     5.10.1 Strict Resource Provisioning 97
     5.10.2 Dynamic Resource Provisioning 100
     5.10.3 Direct Channel Allocation 102
     5.10.4 Summary 105
5.11 Combining Mechanisms 105
5.12 Summary 107

6   **Vulnerabilities in Cellular Data Networks** 109
6.1   History and Description 110
6.2   Delivering Packets from the Internet 111
     6.2.1   Device Registration 111
     6.2.2   Submitting Packets 112
     6.2.3   Routing Packets 112
     6.2.4   Wireless Delivery 113
6.3   Packet Multiplexing 115
6.4   Exploiting Cellular Data Services 116
     6.4.1   Determining Network Settings 116
     6.4.2   Exploiting Teardown Mechanisms 117
     6.4.3   Exploiting Setup Mechanisms 121
6.5   Conflicts in Network Design 124
6.6   Efficient Mitigation of Data Network Vulnerabilities 129
6.7   Summary 130

7   **Vulnerabilities in Voice over IP** 133
7.1   History and Description 134
7.2   Session Initiation Protocol 135
     7.2.1   Architecture 135
     7.2.2   SIP Messages 136

7.2.3   Making Phone Calls 139
7.3   IP-Multimedia Subsystem Network 140
    7.3.1   IMS Architecture................................. 140
    7.3.2   Making Phone Calls 141
7.4   IMS Versus Pure Internet Telephony 141
7.5   Wireless Issues 142
7.6   Security Issues 144
    7.6.1   Current Solutions 145
    7.6.2   Analysis of Emerging Vulnerabilities 148
7.7   Building Secure IP Telephony Networks 152
7.8   Summary.. 153

Part III Future Analyses

8   **Future Directions and Challenges** 157
8.1   Denial of Service Attacks 157
    8.1.1   Logical vs Flooding Attacks 157
    8.1.2   Problems in "Controlled" Networks................. 158
8.2   End-To-End Arguments and Security 159
8.3   The Future of Rigid Systems............................. 160
8.4   Moving Forward....................................... 161

Glossary 163

References 167

Index 179

1

Introduction

Telecommunications networks, and in particular cellular networks, are poised to become the single most important vehicle for communication on earth. From farmers in Mongolia to CEOs in Manhattan, these networks have become essential to business and social interaction. Instantaneous and inexpensive global-scale communication has not only improved our ability to interact with each other, but has also served as the catalyst for new industry, research and discovery. As a result, our standard of living, quality of life and understanding of the world around us have all been improved.

Sadly, as telecommunications networks and the services they support continue to expand and connect greater numbers of people, so too grow the opportunities and motivations for subverting them. It is precisely the essential nature of these networks that make them such an attractive target–adversaries seek to exploit user dependency on the communication media and services to maliciously extracting value and disrupt legitimate activities. The challenge before the technical community is to ensure that these networks operate well in the face of often sophisticated, motivated and well funded adversaries. Tragically, such ends will not be easily achieved. Secure systems and network design is a emerging field whose basic principles are still being defined.

This book documents the still emerging state of security in telecommunications networks. The following chapters focus on the identification and analysis of vulnerabilities in current networks, and explore the underlying causes of these problems. In particular, we focus on the interactions between traditional voice networks (the phone system) and the Internet. We find that such interactions introduce unintended consequences that can effect the fidelity and availability of the network. The latter chapters further detail the state of the art of security solutions for telecommunications networks. However, as a community, we know less about solutions to security. Detailed herein, there are a number of open problems that must be answered before the network will provide the kinds of safety that is needed for users and applications to reach their full potential as a trustworthy global medium. The techniques and solutions identified throughout can serve as a starting point for this analysis.

1.1 Telecommunications Networks

A telecommunications network is a collection of diverse media supporting communication between end-points. Such networks are maintained by *providers* who deploy physical equipment and configure and monitor the network. Individual users or enterprise *customers* subscribe to the service (typically as guided by some financial arrangement). Thereafter the they can access the network to communicate analog (e.g., voice) or digital data to other subscribers. Such communication may cross organizational or provider borders (to other provider networks), and may access services and content through either the telephonic network or the Internet. While definition of telecommunications networks has a broader meaning, this book focuses on the telecommunications networks emerging from traditional phone network. As such, the providers are often phone, wireless, or cable companies.

One may be tempted to assume that telecommunications networks are built upon a single network protocol stack. Nothing could be further from the truth. Unlike the traditional Internet (which is largely built on the IP protocol stack), telecommunications networks are built on a hybrid of physical access media, wireless and wired protocols, and a huge diversity of network equipment. The resulting alphabet soup of standards and devices is often the source of considerable source of confusion, and often serves as a barrier to entry for engineers and scientists.[1] However, as we shall see, underlying all of the complexity is a network who behaves in many ways like the data networks studied in research labs and taught in computer science classes.

Interestingly, much of the current Internet infrastructure grew out of the copper-wire telecommunications phone network deployed in the early part of the twentieth century. The the original AT&T "Ma Bell" telephone company developed and deployed the first commercial digital networks in the 1970s. AT&T spun-off regional telecommunication carriers such as the BellSouth and Pacific Telesys (Pac-Bell) in 1984 in a U.S. government mandated divestiture. During decades of further spin-offs and mergers, these and other providers have continually augmented the physical phone network facilities with data network equipment to build an interconnected global digital networking system. Directly and indirectly, these major providers supply Internet access to home and enterprise customers, and work in concert to control much of the Internet *core*. Note that while traditional analog voice systems are giving way to digital services (e.g., *voice-over-IP*), the "copper-to-the-home" network continues to exist (and will for some time).

Initially deployed at scale in the early 1990s, cellular systems again changed the communication landscape by providing ubiquitous and untethered access to voice services. Digital services such as text messaging were introduced in

---

[1] We attempt to clarify much of this confusion throughout. Chapter 3 presents a in depth discourse on telecommunications standards, which should be viewed as essential reading for readers that lack knowledge of telecommunications system.

the mid to late 1990s and general network access such as provider by EDGE were made available in 2003. Higher bandwidth communications via third generation (3G) systems is now almost universally available. Current cell phones now rival the desktop counterparts in terms of computing and storage capacity. The resources and the services of ubiquitous network availability give rise to new applications and services. The substance and implementation of these applications and services is an active area of investigation.

1.2 Network Convergence and Security

The incredible growth of mobile telecommunications networks as a primary transport for voice and data over the last decade has come as a surprise to even the most ardent visionary. We have only begun to see the impact of these networks--future applications enabled by these networks will far exceed simple voice and text messages. These applications will, for example, support more convenient and secure banking, localized services, and provide near universal access to information services. However, a key technological hurdle remains; how will the network adequately secure the signaling and data for these new applications and environments?

Consider the growing use of cell-phones as a vehicle for "point-of-sale" transactions. As seen in Asia and Europe, the cell phone interacts with the network to support the credit transaction by mediating communication between the vendor, customer, and bank [140, 171, 109]. Such interactions are a substantial departure from traditional closed telephony in that they invite untrusted parties and devices to directly access the network resources in unpredictable ways. Moreover, the banking application may place new requirements on the network—for example, it may be highly desirable (or required) to validate the cell-phone's true identity and the physical location of the purchaser prior to approving the transaction. Standards for current and future networks have not meaningfully addressed these requirements. Thus, the deployment of novel and important applications will be slowed and users unnecessarily exposed to risk. Many of the security lessons learned in one type of network often can not be directly applied to others. Further, as detailed in considerable depth in the following pages, the assumptions built into many systems can unknowingly increase the vulnerability of those systems to attack.

We are in a unprecedented point in the history of network security. We know that the next generation of telecommunications networks is going to serve as the basis for a myriad of critical personal, enterprise, and public services. In short, we know that they will form a significant portion of the Internet. The standards for that new infrastructure are still evolving. What makes this such a unique opportunity is that the technical community can *build security into this new Internet* by reflecting the needs of current and future systems in those standards. To fail in this endeavor will force the world to endure in yet another morass of insecurity, compromise, and system instability. Success in this endeavor will usher in a new generation of trustworthy applications and services. It is our fervent hope that this book will in some small way help take a step toward the latter result.

1.3 Outline of this Book

This book contains 3 parts. Part 1 provides motivation and the technical background needed to understand the book content. Part 2 details the current understanding of security vulnerabilities in telecommunications networks. Part 3 concludes by positing on the future problems and solutions in telecommunications networks. We provide more in-depth detail on the content, structure and intent of these discourses below.

Part 1 details the service and structure of the telecommunications networks, and provides background on the goals and operation of security. The chapter included in this part are:

Chapter 1 − Introduction is this chapter. We give a brief overview of the motivation for the importance of telecommunications security and provide some instruction into the structure and use of the material placed within these pages.

Chapter 3 − Cellular Architecture - provides an overview of the architecture of GSM cellular networks in sufficient depth to understand the vulnerabilities present in current deployments. The prose explores the history of cellular networks as a means of understanding its structure of the network. The core network elements both voice and data communications are identified and example services identified.

Chapter 2 − Security presents the basics of security and describe technology and concepts necessary to understand and evaluate the security problems emerging in cellular and telecommunications networks.

Part 2 of this book presents the known vulnerabilities and weaknesses in telecommunications networks. Through these vulnerabilities, we demonstrate the methodological techniques for used to characterize their scope, severity and difficultly of exploiting these attacks.

Chapter 4 − Vulnerabilities in the Telephony describes general vulnerabilities in telecommunications systems. Such vulnerabilities include the collapse of proprietary cryptographic algorithms, the lack of authenticated messages between elements in the network core, and the growing pool of smart phone-based malware [186].

Chapter 5 − Vulnerabilities in the Short Messaging Service (SMS) describes the canonical telecommunications vulnerability, the SMS attack [184, 61, 183, 182]. This attack exploits the improper use of signaling channels to deliver data traffic (text messages). The chapter describes how a sophisticated adversary can craft an highly effective attack on the network based on targeted forensic analysis. The chapter further characterizes network layer countermeasures that attempt to mitigate the attacks.

Chapter 6 – Vulnerabilities in Cellular Data Networks extends the analysis to high-speed cellular data services. A thorough description of packet delivery, including the processes associated with device setup is given, and vulnerabilities is explored. Analysis of these technologies shows that call setup and tear-down mechanisms designed for "voice-only" traffic can be exploited by data services to mount substantial denial of service attacks [185, 181]. Several mitigation techniques are discussed.

Chapter 7 – Vulnerabilities in Voice over IP presents an overview of VoIP and the protocols and architectures supporting it in both next generation telecommunications net- works and the current Internet. We then explore the Session Initiation Protocol (SIP), its current security mechanisms and their shortcomings in depth, and conclude by considering techniques and architectures for securing VoIP.

Part 3 concludes by discussing the open problems and challenges presented by the current and next generation networks. This part consists of a single chapter, as follows:

Chapter 8 – Future Directions and Challenges posits on the future of telecommunications networks. Centrally, we believe that the next generation of networks will be faced with increasingly hostile and sophisticated adversaries. Thus, the viability of the closed-network assumptions upon which the majority of these networks are build will continue to dissolve. Unless properly addressed, the resulting vulnerabilities will have acute social, technical and financial consequences.

1.4 Audience

The intended audience of this book is computer and network literate readers. No background on telecommunications networks is needed, but some experience with network protocols will be helpful in understanding the book content. An undergraduate degree in computer science or related discipline or experience in the field of network or information security is appropriate preparation for reading this book.

Readers without a background in security are strongly encouraged to read Chapter 2, which provides a working knowledge and lexicon of security appropriate for this book. Similarly, readers who do not have a working understanding of cellular networks or are unaware of more recent standards for the 2, 2.5, and 3G networks are encouraged to read the background in Chapter 3.

1.5 Other Sources of Information

While this book is self-contained, we acknowledge the many valuable resources available on the related topics. Such sources include:

- The Third Generation Partnership Plan (3GPP) Standards [179]

- The Third Generation Partnership Plan 2 (3GPP2) Standards [178]

- The International Telecommunications Union (ITU) [90]

- The Internet Engineering Task Force [174]

- 3G Americas [5]

Part I

Network Architecture

2

Security

2.1 Overview

In this chapter we present the basics of security and decribe technology and concepts necessary to understand and evaluate the security problems emerging in cellular and telecommunications networks. We begin in the next section by asking the million dollar question — what do we *mean* by security?

2.1.1 What is security?

Expectation is the heart of security. A system that behaves as expected is said to be secure. A cellular system that allows calls, prevents its providers and users from being defrauded, and maintains an acceptable quality of service throughout would therefore be deemed secure. In some sense, this sounds very much like a definition of the behavior of the *any* reasonable phone system, secure or not. Where security extends a system's functional requirements is in defining the *adversary*.

An adversary (also known as hacker, attacker, ...) is an entity attempting undermine the quality or content of the system under scrutiny. When evaluating security, one defines what the powers of the adversary are expected to be. So, a system is said to be secure only if it prevents the assumed adversary from harming the system. Of course, it is a practical impossibility to be secure against all possible adversairess—omni-present, all knowing adversaries will be able to prevent the system from performing correctly with near certainty. Security is therefore a game of understanding realistic adversaries and designing systems to prevent them from doing harm. Surprisingly, anticipating what those harms are turns out to be half the battle.

A more precise definition of security is that it defines the requirements *authenticity, availability, fidelity,* and *privacy* of the information it serves. Authenticity speaks to the origins of information, and indicates that the data received as intended by the legitimate users of the system. For example, in many networks, it is important that the billing of the information is correct, i.e., is authentic. Availability and fidelity are closely related topics that indicate that the data is accesible and the access is of sufficient quality to be useful. The obvious example of this is a voice call; inability to have a coherent voice conversation represents a serious failure of the network. Where such failures are intentionally caused by an adversary, this represents a failure of security.

Privacy is a surprisingly controversial dimension of security. Most often users wish their communications (e.g., voice and data communications) and behaviors (e.g., call records, network usage, physical location) to be only available to those they explicitly authorize. Of course, the providers also wish to prevent access to user data, but are subject to local laws and need to share such information internally to manage the network.

As will be demonstrated throughout the following chapters, allocating the appropriate due protections is an exercise in tradeoffs. Introducing too much security can be costly and inhibit proper operation. Placing too little can spell disaster.

2.1.2 Basic Terminology

Before delving into the details of how one evaluates and addresses security, we introduce terminology used throughout. As is true of many areas of technology, terminology is not perfectly coordinated between all standards, texts, and uses. This reality has served to complicate an already murky lexicon. We will try to identify common terminological issues throughout. Lets start with the basics.

- *Principals* - principals are the legitimate actors in any system. Depending on the context, principals can be machines or organizations. The central principals in the telephony networks are the customers (cellular and POTS users) and providers.
- *Credentials* - Credentials are the artifacts that provide identity. For example, in the physical world, one can use a driver's license as a credential. In computer systems, such credentials are typically manifest as passwords or cryptographic keys.
- *Authentication* - this is the process by which an identity is associated with some principal. This is typically accomplished by the principal providing or proving possession of some credential.
- *Authorization* - authorization determines which rights a principal possesses. For example, a cell phone owner may have calling plan that provides access to some services, but not others. The cellular network governs access to services by looking up which service the system is authorized to access.
- *Transport Security* - sometimes called transit security, is the process of protecting communications as it traverses an untrusted network. This is

commonly accomplished by using cryptography to ensure confidentiality and integrity, among other properties.

- *Vulnerabilities* - vulnerabilities are artifacts of a system that allow the security of the system to be subverted. Software bugs, failure to recognize potential misuse, and open functionality lead to vulnerabilities. These are the vectors and adversary uses to compromise a system.
- *Countermeasures* - countermeasures are elements in the the system (or its design) that address specific threats against the system. For example, phone networks restrict the amount of VOIP calls that can arrive from external sources. Such a countermeasure prevents the flooding of the phone network from adversaries on the Internet.

2.1.3 Attacks

Attacks occur when a vulnerability is exploited by an adversary. Whether it is by exploiting a buffer overflow to compromise a desktop operating system, or by flooding a network with traffic, they all serve to accomplish some mal-intent by the adversary. Attacks can be broadly classified into three categories based on *how* they accomplish the nefarious goals.

Adversaries mount an *active attack* by manipulating the target system (or its supporting infrastructure) directly. Attacks in this class send forged messages, modify internal or external data, and/or prevent legitimate activities from occurring. Note that the adversary must interact with the system in some way–which is beneficial in a sense because it provides some behavior for detection.

Conversely, adversaries of *passive attacks* do not interact with the system directly. Like a restaurant customer at a nearby table who listens in to your dinner conversation, passive adversaries simply observe. In the phone system context, such attacks typically involve the adversary *eavesdropping* voice conversations, call setup signaling, or billing data.

Denial of service (DOS) attacks are a sub-class of active attacks that attempt to incapacitate or reduce the quality of response of the system. Attacks of this type occur commonly on the Internet–websites providing content which adversaries do not want seen are "taken down" by flooding the associated server with bogus or replicated requests.

2.1.4 Trust

Interestingly, one of the most important aspects of security is often the least well-defined: *trust*. Trust is the expectation of a principal to act in an anticipated manner. For example, one the phone company to provide service if you pay your bill. As in private life, such trust is rarely absolute, sometimes not symmetric, almost never transitive, and subject to change.

Assessing trust is key to developing a coherent security strategy. One needs to understand who we trust to perform (and not perform) actions and under what circumstances to determine which attacks the system needs to be resilient to. Of course, prudence dictates that one needs to carefully evaluate those cases where trust may be mistakenly misplaced.

A trust model is an explicit assessment of the trust embodied in the system. The trust model is a blueprint security; one places security infrastructure that is necessary to preserve the trust relationships. Of course, developing a complete (or even comprehensive) trust model for something as complex as the phone network is very difficult, and in some case impractical.

2.2 Services and Tools

This section reviews the basic technologies and tools used to secure telecommunications and other networks.

2.2.1 Cryptography

Cryptography is the art of secret writing. Historically, the tools of cryptography were used to hide the content of military or diplomatic missives, and many cases used in the conduct of any number of conpiracies [103]. Shortly after the beginning of the information age, public computers and networks were processing and transmitting information of incredible personal or organizational value. It became clear that the owners of that information required that the data be protected. Cryptography was the solution.

Thus, the modern age of cryptography was born. Today, modern cryptographic algorithms protect, among many other artifacts, network communications and the files we store on local hard drives. Algorithms implementing cryptography exist in almost every electronic device one can think of. Laptops, cellphones, cable-television boxes, and many other devices all employ the protections afforded cryptography. Such algorithms work in concert to provide privacy (e.g., of cellular calls), implement digital rights management, and a myriad of other services essential to electronic services.

Cryptography is a small part of security. While it is often an essential part of providing security, it is not a mechanism for providing in and of itself—one needs to select and use the cryptographic algorithms carefully to ensure that desired security requirements are provided. Many of the most dangerous (and costly) vulnerabilities in history are the result of the poor application of cryptography.

Cryptography is a subtle and evolving art. Based in areas of theoretical computer science and mathematics, the study of cryptography is in its infancy. Some areas are more mature (e.g., public key encryption), others are less so (e.g., stegonography). As a system designer or security evaluator, it is important to keep current on the recent advances in the field, as these advances informs how one should use the tools that are available.

One might be tempted to develop custom or proprietary cryptographic algorithms–*this urge should be resisted at all costs*. Becoming conversant in the techniques and pitfalls of cryptographic designs takes even the most talented mathematicians and scientists years. The technical industry is littered with companies that suffered the (often commercially fatal) consequences of broken "home-brewed" cryptography. We dicuss a particularly damaging violation of this canon in the design of the COMP128 algorithm in Chapter 4

Symmetric Key Cryptography

Dating back to the days of Caesar and before, two parties who desire to communicate confidentially have traditionally used a symmetric key (or shared key) key algorithm. This algorithm is defined as the pair of functions,

$$E(k, m) = c \qquad D(k, c) = m,$$

or alternatively,

$$D(k, E(k, m)) = m,$$

where $E()$ is an encryption function, $D()$ is the decryption function, m is the the *plaintext* message, c is the *ciphertext*, and k is a secret key. This algorithm is also known as a cipher.

When in use in computer systems, the message typically is the data to be sent between computers. For example, it could be an SMS or email message. The ciphertext is a random-looking string of bytes determined by the encryption algorithm. The ciphertext is transmitted from the sender to the receiver using whatever media is appropriate. Access to the plaintext is indirectly governed by access to the key–anyone who has access to the key can simply decrypt the message using $D()$.

What makes such an algorithm "secure" is the difficulty of determining the message without the key. Note that in security, one assumes that the adversary has access to the cryptographic algorithms, but not they key. Known as Kirkoff's principal, this reflects the reality that each algorithm is explicitly exposed in the executable code implementing that algorithm. Preventing access to that code in perpetuity is in almost all cases practically impossible.

There are two kinds of symmetric key algorithms; *stream ciphers* and *block ciphers* . Stream ciphers receive input as a continuos stream of input plaintext or ciphertext bytes and output a continuous stream of ciphertext or plaintext, respectively. Conversely, block ciphers accept fixed width input (in bytes, typically) and fixed output; the width of which is the *block size*.

Introduced in the 1976, the data encryption standard (DES) [130] remained until recently the most widely used symmetric algorithm. However, because of its small key size (56 bits), it can be compromised by brute force–it is now feasible to "guess" the key by trying all 2^{56} of them with commodity hardware in a relatively short time. The triple DES algorithm (3DES) [134] was created to extend the lifetime of DES by using multiple keys and increase the effective key size to 122 bits. However, because it slow, 3DES is viewed as unattractive for many applications.

A NIST-sponsored effort to replace the the aging DES algorithm was launched in the 1990s. The resulting Advanced Encryption Standard (AES) [137] was finalized in 2001. This is currently the de-facto standard for symmetric key cryptography in networks and systems.

Public Key Cryptography

Public key cryptography (or alternately asymmetric key cryptography) allows parties achieve confidentiality without sharing a secret. Each party in these systems uses a key generation algorithm to create two keys, a public key (k^+) and a private key (k^-). Both keys are used for encrypting data.

What distinguishes public key systems from shared secret systems is that anything encrypted with the public key can *only* be decrypted using the private key and anything encrypted with the private key can *only* be decrypted using the public key, i.e., the keys serve as encryption inverses of each other:

$$D(k^+, E(k^-, m)) = m,$$
$$D(k^-, E(k^+, m)) = m$$

In practice, the owner of a (k^+, k^-) *key pair* will freely distribute the public key, but keep the secret key confidential. Thus, anyone who desires to speak to that owner need only obtain the public key, encrypt the message using that key, and transmit the resulting ciphertext to the owner. Because only the owner knows the private key, he is the only one who can recover the original plaintext; therefore, eavesdropping the transmission is of no value to an adversary. The RSA algorithm [153] is the most widely used public key algorithm.

Hashing, Integrity and Message Authentication

A *cryptographic hash function* is a foundational tool of cryptography that creates "fingerprints" of data. These functions accept inputs of varying sizes and return a single, fixed-size (128 or 196 bits in popular algorithms) "hash" of the data. A hash of a message m would is calculated as:

$$H(m) = x$$

Cryptographic hash algorithms must be non-invertible and collision resistant. Non-invertablity is the property that one should not be able reverse the algorithm and retrieve the original data (pre-image) from the hash output. Collision resistance is the property that it should be infeasible to find two inputs that result in the same output. The two most popular algorithms are the MD5 [152] and SHA-1[1] [58] algorithms.

---

[1] SHA-1 has recently been found to be significantly weaker than originally though, possibly fatally so.

Hash algorithms are used principally in guaranteeing the integrity of data. For example, a *message authentication code* (MAC) is an integrity proving construction that uses symmetric keys. Also known as a *keyed hash* (and to simplify somewhat), this approach simply hashes a concatenation of the shared key and the message:

$$H(k|m) = x$$

The resulting MAC x is then transmitted with the message to the receiver (who is the party with whom the key is shared). Upon the reception of the message, the receiver computes the MAC by performing the above operation on the shared key and the received message. If the received MAC is the same as the MAC computed, then the integrity of the message is verified (because you must have the key to create a correct MAC). Note that the MAC also vouches for the authenticity of the message, e.g., because the recipient and the sender are the only parties who know the key, then it can securely attribute the message to the sender.

The public key analog to a MAC is a digital signature. The *signer* of uses its private key on a signing algorithm to create the signature. Anyone who desires to validate that signature can do so free thereafter by applying the signature validation algorithm to the message, the signature, and the signer's public key, as such:

$$Sign(k^-, m) = sig(x),$$
$$Validate(k^+, m, sig(x)) = \{valid, invalid\},$$

Note that the owner of the public key need not have any knowledge of those who would be validating the data. This is an enormously useful feature to have in building secure systems.

2.2.2 Authentication and Authorization

An authentication process establishes the identity of some entity under scrutiny. For example, the most widely used form of authentication is the password; anyone who can produce a password associated with a user ID is allowed to assume that identity. Hence, the security of the protected system is determined by how "guessable" that password is.

The evidence produced to prove identity during authentication is called a *credential*. Credentials can be you you know (e.g., passwords, social security numbers), something you have (e.g., key-cards, security tokens, SecureIDs), or something you are (e.g., biometrics via eye-scans, finger prints, etc.). Sometimes two or more different methods of authentication are used. This *multi-factor authentication* is used to amplify the security provided by often weaker forms of authentication, e.g., new standards for online banking require the user provide both a password and proof of possesion of a security token.

Successful authentication does not imply that the authenticated entity is a priori given access. An *authorization* process uses authentication, possibly with other information, to make decisions about whom to give access. An *access control* system makes decisions about what rights an entity has within the confines of the governed system. For example, the ability of a user on a UNIX system to modify files is restricted by the UNIX access control policy to that which is stated in the RWX "access bits" associated with them.

2.2.3 Certificates and PKI

A digital certificate is a signed data structure that makes an association between an identity and a public key. This is said to *bind* the key to the user. Certificates are most frequently used for authentication (via proving knowledge of the private key) and for committments (via digtal signature).

Certificates are *issued* by *Certification Authorities* (CA). The CA issues a certificate by signing an identity (e.g., user's name, job title, or domain), validity dates, the public key, and other information. A user validates a received certificate by checking the included digital signature using the CA's public key. The CA's public key is assumed to be freely distributed (or potentially issued by some other CA that is). In its most general form, a system used to distribute and validate certificates is called a public key infrastructure (PKI).

Consider the PKI used to validate websites on the Internet. Most web browsers are installed with a collection of CA certificates that are invariantly trusted (i.e. do not need to be validated). Many web sites publish certificates issued by the Verisign CA (Verisign, 2002) whose certificate is installed with most browsers. When a user retrieves a certificate from a website as part of negotiating a secure session (using SSL/TLS–see Section 2.3.2), it checks the local cache of CA certificates. If the signing CA is in the cache and the certificate validates correctly, then the certificate is accepted as being authentic. The user is then presented with some indicator of success (often a "key" icon somewhere on the display) to indicate that the broswer has successfully authenticated the website.

2.3 Network Security

Like other areas in security, network security can be defined the protections and detections it employs. We begin a review of these methods by detailing the current approaches to transport security and their applications (e.g., VPNs), then detail methods for filtering (e.g., firewalls) and monitoring and identification of malcious activity (e.g., intrusion detection).

2.3.1 IPsec

A transport security solution is a layer of protocols (called a suite) that provides communication security functionality to applications or services in a

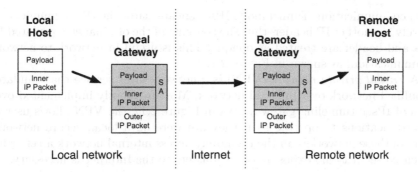

Fig. 2.1. IPsec Tunneling - sender datagrams, including headers, are securely encapsulated (e.g., via encryption) as it traverses an IPsec gateway on the edge of a local network. The reverse transform is performed and the ingress edge of the remote network, and thereafter forwarded to the end host. Eavesdroppers on the Internet cannot ascertain anything more that traffic is passing between the networks.

transparent or near transparent manner. The IPsec protocol suite [107] is a implementation of such security within the IP protocols. Thus, all IP datagrams passing between IPsec-enabled hosts are "transformed" (for example via encryption) to ensure that the security properties agreed upon by the hosts are preserved. In particular, the confidentiality, integrity, authenticity of each such packet may guaranteed.

IPsec occurs in 2 stages. The first time that two hosts exchange a packet, they must establish cryptographic keys and agree on what security properties are appropriate for the communication. This first stage is implemented by the Internet Key Exchange protocol (IKE) [84]. The hosts use IKE to mutually authenticate each other using a range of credentials (e.g., passwords, certificates), negotiate a shared key, and establish a set of guidelines dictating what security guarantees are needed and the means by which they are achieved (the security policy). This collection of information is called an *IPsec security association*, and is stored in at each host within the security association database (SADB). Note that SAs are uni-directional. Thus, a pair of hosts will establish 2 SAs (one in each direction) to support bi-directional communication.

The second stage of IPsec is the steady-state processing of datagrams. There are two protocols used to transform the datagrams passing between hosts (precisely one is selected for each SA); the *Authentication Header* (AH) [105] and the *Encapsulating Security Payload* (ESP) [106]. To simplify, AH provides authenticity and integrity, and ESP provides authenticity, integrity, and confidentiality. The protocols are configured via the SA policy with a cipher suite of cryptographic protocols, which indicates which particular ciphers and algorithms used to implement security, e.g., DES and SHA-1.

IPsec can operate in either transport or tunnel mode. In transport mode, the payload of the data is encrypted, but the IP headers are largely left in tact. This is the mode that is commonly used to implement IP *end-to-end* (host-to-host) communication. Tunnel mode IPsec encapsulates the IP communication entirely in another IP header–thus the contents of the original encapsulated IP data and header are treated as opaque. This is useful in network-to-network communication, as shown in Figure 2.1.

A *virutal private network* (VPN) is a network layer service that emulates a confined network over physical network. Most frequently implemented over pairs of IPsec tunneling gateways (as in Figure 2.1), the VPN allows user in remote locations to operate as if they are were on a local, secure network. Users of these networks can then remotely access internal network assets with increased security–no exposure of such assets to the Internet is necessary.

2.3.2 SSL/TLS

In contrast to IPsec, the Secure Sockets Layer (SSL) protocol and its successor Transport Layer Security (TLS) provide security at the application layer. The principle use of SSL and TLS is in the securing of Internet communication–most notably securing the communication of web traffic, instant messaging, email, and other user applications. Implementations of SSL such as OpenSSL [3] have been developed and are widely used. The popularity of the protocol is largely a reflection of its ease of use. Once invoked, all of the details of negotiating and implementing security are largely transparent to the programmer. For this reason, SSL/TLS have been widely used to provide security in telecommunications applications such as VOIP (see Chapter 7).

SSL and TLS provide for the negotiation of security parameters, the establishment of symmetric session keys, and the securing of data passed between the *peers*. The protocols provide–among other properties–confidentiality, integrity, authenticity and replay protections.

The structure of the interactions of SSL/TLS largely mirrors that of IPSec. The peers initially signal their desire to securely communucate via an exchange of "hello" messages. The client and server then exchange proposals for the policy to be used to guide the session, e.g., the ciphers, MAC, timeouts, etc. Once they reach agreement, the peers securely exchange seed information used to generate the symmetric session keys. The parties compute the session keys and signal an end to the negotiation exchanges. Thereafter they can exchange application data. The payloads of the application messages are encrypted and MACed as defined by policy. At the termination of the session, the peers gracefully abandon the session by sending a "goodbye" message.

Certificates are used to authenticate peers. However, in many situations (and by default in many instances) only the receiver (server) of the connection is authenticated. The reason for this is that often the server is dealing with anonymous clients. For example, consider the web server serving commercial content. The client may wish to purchase goods but may not have a certificate or any association with a CA to obtain one. This arrangement is perfectly acceptable, as the the client will eventually be authenticated via some other means (e.g., via a credit card number). In practice, the complexity and security

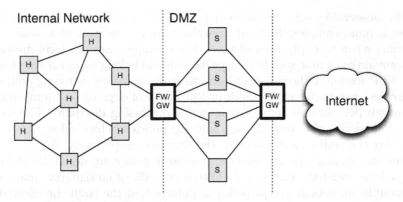

Fig. 2.2. Firewall/DMZ usage - firewalls (FW) are placed at the gateways (GW) between enterprise networks and the Internet (or provider) to prevent unwanted traffic from entering. Those enterprises which need provide access to internal resources place services (S) in an enclosed DMZ network. The gateway between the DMZ and the internal network will tightly police the traffic passing through it towards enterprise hosts (H).

requirements of generating *client-side* certificates has proven to be simply too high for most applications. Thus, they have not seen much adoption for large scale applications such as the web, email, and instant messaging. However, other (more closed) applications such as online banking have embraced client certificates, and provide the infrastructure for acquiring and using them.

2.3.3 Firewalls

Firewalls are a means to isolate one security domain (e.g., application, network) from another. Firewalls are placed an ingress and egress points of a network, host, or application. Traffic crossing the interface that matches a defined signature is handled according to the specified policy, e.g., dropped.

Network layer firewalls (also known as packet filters) are often placed at the gateway between a network and the Internet or provider network. They are used to govern which hosts inside the network can be reached or can send traffic to external networks. For example, Figure 2.2 shows a common network topology. Often it is essential enterprises to have hosts that are *Internet-facing*, i.e., hosts that are reachable from anywhere on the network. It is advantageous to place these hosts in a intermediate network called a *DMZ*. The firewalls at the border with the Internet allow traffic to hosts in the DMZ, but not into the internal network. The firewall policy at the gateway between the DMZ and the internal network is carefully constructed to defend the internal network against potentially compromised services.

Firewalls are driven by their policy. The matching policy, e.g., signature, defines which traffic should be processed. Often this is a simple attribute that is easily observable, e.g., destination port or IP address. Other times, the process is more complex. Stateful firewalls monitor the state of a session to determine when to apply firewall rules. For example, network level firewalls often provide rules that specify that packets should belong to an existing legitimate TCP session. Other kinds of firewalls have analogous matching policies, and are designed to detect the kinds or legitimacy of ongoing communication.

Firewall policies also define the intended processing discipline. The most basic of these are the *accept*, *deny*, and *log* policies, which allow, drop, or simply log the traffic as it traverses the firewalls, respectively. Again, more complex and domain specific policies processing policy are available. *Default policies* define what the firewall should to with traffic if no signature matches. For example, an default-accept policy stipulates that the traffic be allowed if no signature is detected. Default-deny policies are generally considered more secure, in that it requires all traffic be intentionally allowed.

Firewalls can be placed at any layer in the protocol stack–from the physical layer all the way to application layer. In particular, application level firewalls are proving to be a effective way to cleanse input from untrusted sources, and are now common in web systems. Firewalls may either proxy traffic or be transparent. Proxy firewalls terminate the connection, and proxy the traffic toward the destination. This is useful where you have sensitive services that you want to prevent external parities from directly communicating with, e.g., sensitive databases. Transparent firewalls are just that; they process the traffic and forward it as dictated by policy. For example, the network layer firewalls in Figure 2.2 are transparent–the leave allowed traffic unmolested.

2.3.4 Intrusion and Anomaly Detection

An intrusion detection system (IDS) monitors the state of a system and attempts to identify malicious activity occurring on it. The IDS system collects data via sensors. Using signatures or other models of behavior it determines are certain events represent malicious activity based on the sensor input. These systems create an *alarm* in response to the detected activity. Attacks that are correctly detected are *true positives*, and those that are not are *false negatives*. Conversely, non-attack events that are incorrectly labeled as attacks are *false positives*, and those that are not are *true negatives*.

Alarms are generally delivered to some observation point for processing, e.g., a network operation center (NOC). What is done in response to the observation of that alarm is determined by the nature of the event and the environment in which it is detected. An intrusion prevention system (IPS) automatically reacts to an alarm by placing additional countermeasures, to reconfigure the system, or place additional sensors.

A *network intrusion detection system* (NIDS) is an intrusion detection system that monitors the state of a network for malicious activity such as denial of service attacks or worm behavior. Consider a *port scanning*[2] NIDS. A simple *attack signature* would look for many connection attempts by a single host. In implementing this signature, the NIDS would monitor all connections attempted by all hosts within the network (a non-trivial task), and signal an alarm if the connection attempts spread across a threshold of unique ports. Note that this signature is imperfect: if the ports are scanned by multiple hosts or very slowly (such that the previous connection attempts are flushed out of the monitoring state), then such an attack will not be detected.

Anomaly-based intrusion detection systems monitor the state of the system or network by modeling anomalous behavior (as opposed to modeling normal behavior). These system do not use signatures, but rather apply heuristics or rules to identify anomalous events. The chief advantage of this approach is that it can detect previously unknown attacks. The challenge is therefore in learning what an anomaly is.

Learning techniques are used by IDS to develop detection signatures and heuristics, which are models of attack or normal behavior. These approaches range from simple statistical evaluation to complex machine learning algorithms. Generally, these system use historical data to *train* the IDS system, i.e., to develop the attack models. Systems that have examples of known examples of events to be detected are said to use *supervised learning*, and those without examples use *unsupervised learning*.

An irony of an intrusion detection system is that detection accuracy only partially effects the success of a IDS. What often is important is the rate of *false positives*, i.e., the rate at which normal events are incorrectly labeled as attacks. Suppose that there is one attack event in every 10,000 (This is reasonable in many environments because most traffic is not malicious) and the system implements a 99% accurate detection algorithm, .i.e.:

$$Pr(alarm|attack) = 0.99$$
$$Pr(alarm|!attack) = 0.01$$
$$Pr(attack) = 0.0001$$
$$Pr(!attack) = 0.9999$$

From this we can calculate the probability of an arbitrary event generating alarm in this environment:

$$Pr(alarm) = Pr(alarm|attack) * Pr(attack) + Pr(alarm|!attack) * Pr(!attack)$$
$$= (0.99 * 0.0001) + (0.01 * 0.9999)$$
$$= (0.000099) + (0.009999)$$
$$= 0.010098$$

Next we can apply Bayes rule to determine the probability that a given alarm represents a real attack:

---

[2] A *port scanning* attack is a form of reconnaissance used by adversaries to map the available services within a network by attempting to connect to ranges of port numbers, and recording which attempts are successful.

$$Pr(attack|alarm) = \frac{Pr(alarm|attack) * Pr(attack)}{Pr(alarm)}$$

$$= \frac{0.99 * 0.0001}{0.010098}$$
$$= 0.0098039216 \approx 1\%$$

Surprisingly, the probability that an intrusion is detected in a system that is 99% accurate detector just less than 1%. This is known as the Base-Rate Fallacy [37]. The intuition is that the failure rate (in false positives) is amplified by the large number of events–because the ratio of "attack" to "normal" is so small. Thus, because of the rarity of real attacks, even a very accurate system is likely to more likely to err on a legitmiate event than it is detect the rare true positive.

A consequence of the Base Rate Fallacy is that suppression of false positives is often the central challenge of building and using an IDS. Much focus has been centered around this challenge, but to date false positives are a still limiting factor in the use of many intrusion detection systems. However, despite the limitations of the technique, NIDS continue to be widely and effectively deployed in enterprise networks.

2.4 Summary

This chapter has provided a brief overview of security including its goals and terminology, the structure and use of cryptography, and the basic tools for securing a network, e.g., IPsec, firewalls, intrusion detection. The scope of this chapter was intended to enable comprehension of the attacks and countermeasures presented in chapters to follow. However, the content in this chapter is not sufficient by itself to understand the true depth and subtlety of information security research and engineering.

Readers interested in obtaining a more in-depth treatment are directed to fuller treatises on the subject. For example, standard textbooks [104, 54] are often a highly useful source of information for terminology and basic techniques. User's seeking more specific and current information about vulnerabilities, designs, and related technologies should review the material provided by public and government organizations such as CERT [1] and NIST [2].

3

Cellular Architecture

For large portions of the world's population, cellular networks represent the only persistent digital connection with the outside world. The combination of device portability, reasonable cost and nearly ubiquitous coverage across an increasing percentage of the globe make the services provided by these networks generally more accessible than those provided by the Internet. While the services have generally been limited in their breadth when compared to the Internet, the increasingly interconnected nature of cellular systems and the Internet will create significant new security issues. In order to understand the implications of this increased connectivity, it is critical that engineers and scientists working in Internet domain are aware of the architecture of cellular systems.

In this chapter, we provide an overview of the architecture of GSM cellular networks. We begin by exploring the history of cellular networks so as to understand the design decisions behind current systems. We then present the core network elements supporting both voice and data communications. These discussions include the reuse of both mechanism and design philosophy throughout the network. Our focus then turns to the network and protocols connecting such elements - the *Signaling System Number 7* (SS7) network. The SS7 architecture is directly compared against the more familiar Internet protocol stack so that readers can easily contrast design decisions. After exploring the wireless portion of the network, we then discuss common network operations including registration and making calls. We finish our discussion be examining current security mechanisms protecting both the core and wireless portions of such network.

A complete treatment of GSM networks is simply not possible outside of reading several thousand pages of standards documents. Accordingly, we intend this chapter to should serve as a jumping-off point for researchers. With a firm understanding of the architecture presented herein, those interested in further exploring additional specific details of both current and next generation networks should consult the documentation available through the *Third Generation Partnership Plan* (3GPP) website [179].

3.1 History of Cellular Telephony

The first analog cellular telephony systems were introduced in the early 1980's. The systems, typified by the *Advanced Mobile Phone System* (AMPS) and the derivative *Total Access Communication System* (TACS) allowed users to receive telephone calls while roaming between systems. System bandwidth was segmented using *Frequency-Division Multiple Access* (FDMA). Bandwidth was broken into many carriers, each of which was capable of supporting a single simplex voice channel. When a call was active, one frequency was used in each direction to allow full duplex communication. Due to propagation characteristics, spatial reuse of frequencies was possible, thus allowing national coverage. These systems were limited in capacity due to inefficiencies of analog voice transport. They were also limited in terms of services due to the use of analog signaling. While largely replaced by more efficient systems, analog cellular networks are still in use across the globe. Products including the OnStar automotive security system [74] and home security systems by ADT [28] and GE Security [73] still rely upon AMPS to communicate with monitoring stations in many areas. Regulatory changes by the FCC permitting cellular providers to cease support for AMPS in early 2008 [68], however, will effectively bring an end to analog cellular systems in the United States.

To overcome these limitations, digital systems, called *Second Generation* (2G) systems were introduced in the early 1990s, most of which are still in use. The first systems combine FDMA with *Time-Division Multiple Access* (TDMA) - each carrier is now also divided into time-slots organized into repeating frames. With these systems, each voice call is assigned a time-slot within a frame. Thus each carrier is capable of supporting multiple calls. Each time slot carries one sample of digitized voice. Because digital transmission allows for redundancy and error correction, transmission at lower power is possible. This enables more aggressive frequency re-use, thus further increasing capacity. The GSM system is the prime example of a TDMA cellular system. GSM originated in Europe and is used in most parts of the world. In the US, a similar system based on the IS-136 standard was introduced. However, most IS-136 will be phased out and fully replaced by GSM by early 2008.

An additional important aspect of these systems was the introduction of digital control channels. These channels allow for a great amount of information exchange between the network and mobile device, thus enabling better security solutions and a richer set of services, such as text messaging.

In parallel with the development of TDMA systems in the US, a second digital system based on *Code-Division Multiple Access* (CDMA) was developed and deployed. While these systems provide seemingly similar services to TDMA systems, they use vastly different wireless technology. These systems are based on the IS-95 series of standards. We explore the differences between FDMA, TDMA and CDMA systems in greater depth in Section 3.5.1.

As cellular voice services matured, the focus of service providers moved to providing mobile data services. With the addition of these services, the

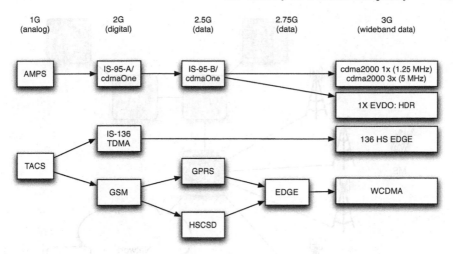

Fig. 3.1. The evolutionary paths of the major telecommunications standards.

so-called "2.5G" networks were deployed. GSM systems were augmented with the *General Packet Radio Service* (GPRS). GPRS provides packet services at data rates of tens of kilobits per second. New modulation techniques called *Enhanced Data Rates for GSM Evolution* (EDGE), often referred to as "2.75G" systems, were introduced to increase these rates to over 200 kbps. CDMA systems were likewise augmented with data services as part of the IS-95B standard.

While theoretically high data rates are possible in 2.5 and 2.75G networks, users typically experience bandwidth comparable to wired dial-up access. *Third Generation* (3G) networks attempt to address this issue through the eventual use of new spectrum and more efficient encoding techniques. However, much of the old core infrastructure will be used at least initially to run such networks. GSM, for instance, is being evolved to the *Universal Mobile Telecommunication System* (UMTS), and will use *Wideband CDMA* (WCDMA) over the air. UMTS promises increased voice capacity and multimedia services with data rates of up to tens of Mbps. IS-95-based systems continue to evolve using narrowband CDMA as part of the CDMA2000 standards. Packet data services at nominal rates of over 10 Mbps are provided using 1xEVDO.

The first, second and early third generation voice systems all re-use the signaling infrastructure of the wired telephone networks. The emerging 3G networks are migrating to Internet-based signaling and services.

We discuss these systems and architecture in more detail below.

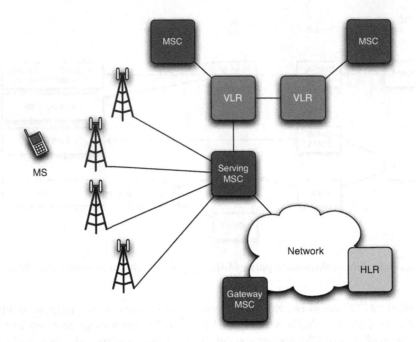

Fig. 3.2. The major components in an SS7 network.

3.2 Cellular Voice Networks

3.2.1 Voice Network Elements

The mobile telecommunication network evolved from the fixed wireline tele-phone network. These networks use highly intelligent switches made up of switch fabrics and highly reliable processing elements. These processors run programs to enact functions such as routing, resource reservation, digit anal-ysis (for activating services), etc. Separate processors, often called adjunct processor or *Network Control Points* (NCPs), store and execute additional programs for services such as 800-number, credit card calls, etc. To build the mobile telecommunications network, these switches and adjunct processors are loaded with additional software to provide the intelligence to perform mobility management.

Mobility management must address two main issues - connections over which communication takes place must be established between endpoints and services must be available to mobile users. In a wireline network these items are straight-forward. Switches store routing tables by which a dialed telephone number may be routed to its destination. Telephone switches that serve fixed phones have access to databases and processors to provide services to their subscribers. In a mobile network, users must first be located before a connec-tion can be completed. A mobile phone number is simply a logical identifier for a phone; it has no strong geographical meaning. This requires the network to track the location of devices and to locate them when a call arrives. Because a user may receive a call through many different switches depending on their current location, service profiles and software must be accessible to all switches in the network.

To achieve these goals the mobile voice network introduces several network elements. A simplified network is shown in Figure 3.2.

3.2.2 Home Location Register

The heart of the mobile network is the *Home Location Register* (HLR). Essentially a massive database, the HLR addresses the issues created by mobility in a phone network by storing permanent copies of user profiles, which contains information including the address of the switch currently providing service to a *Mobile Station* (MS) (a.k.a. a phone). All requests involving the user, from incoming calls to the network determining whether a user is eligible to receive certain services (e.g., call-forwarding), are handled by the HLR. Table 3.1 summarizes the mandatory information stored in an HLR according to the standards documents [15].

One of the most important duties of the HLR is authentication. While standards documents mention the presence of an *Authentication Center* (AuC), the functions of these elements are absorbed by nearly every commercially available HLR. As is standard practice in the field, we therefore refer only to the HLR when such operations are performed. In order to perform its authentication duties, an HLR assigns a unique identifier, known as the *International Mobile Subscriber Identity* (IMSI), and a unique cryptographic key, K_i, to each user in the network. In order to determine whether or not a device should be granted access to the network, the HLR creates a challenge that can only be correctly responded to by the device with the correct K_i on its *Subscriber Identity Module* (SIM) card. The protocol used to actually perform such authentication is discussed in greater detail in Section 3.7.

Device level authentication is also possible in GSM networks using an *Equipment Identity Register* (EIR) – functionality that is also typically absorbed by the HLR. In addition to an IMSI, which is stored in the SIM, each device carries a unique identifier known as the *International Mobile Equipment Identity* (IMEI). Should a device be stolen or be known to be causing harm to the network, the HLR can simply add the IMEI to a blacklist and prevent the device from attaching to the network.

Users are assigned to specific HLRs based on their phone number, allowing queries to be efficiently routed. The number of HLRs in a network, however, is highly variable. Limitations on processing power and the number of concurrent database lookups forced early cellular providers to use many HLRs throughout the network. The advantages to this approach were numerous. For instance, failure in one HLR meant that the majority of the network would remain unaffected. However, the cost of administering and maintaining so

Table 3.1. Mandatory data stored in the HLR and/or VLR.

Data	HLR	VLR	Description
IMSI	✓	✓	Permanent and unique identifier assigned to each user. Different than the user's phone number (MSISDN).
IMEI		✓	Unique identifier for an MS.
TMSI/P-TMSI		✓	Temporary identifier used to preserve the privacy of a user's identity over the air.
NAM	✓		Indicates whether a client is registered to receive voice, data or both services.
MSISDN	✓	✓	Voice phone number for an MS.
RAND/SRES and K_C	✓		Random number, signed response and session key in authentication triplets.
K_i	✓		Encryption key shared between HLR and a specific MS.
VLR Number	✓		Identifies the VLR currently serving an MS.
MSC Number	✓		Identifies the MSC currently serving an MS.
SGSN Number	✓	✓	Identifies the SGSN currently serving an MS.
GGSN Number	✓	✓	Identifies the GGSN currently serving an MS.
Roaming Restricted	✓		Notes that a feature is not supported in an SGSN or MSC and can be used to prevent a device from associating with an LA.
Provision of teleservice	✓	✓	Identifies which services (e.g., voice, SMS, data) an MS is able to receive.
Transfer of SM	✓		Indicates whether a text message should be sent via the voice or data network.
MNRR	✓		Specifies the reason why an MS is not reachable (e.g., not GPRS or IMSI attached).
MS purged for non-GPRS flag	✓		MS information has been removed from the VLR.
MS purged for GPRS flag	✓		MS information has been removed from the SGSN.
GGSN-list	✓		Notes the GGSNs (including their number and IP address) to be contacted if a device is not GPRS attached.

many databases in the face of rising computing power has led to a significant centralization of network resources. A number of large providers have now or are in the process of migrating to a single, network-wide HLR.

If an HLR were to fail or be compromised, especially given the move toward centralization, the corresponding cellular network would simply cease to operate. A successful attack on such a device, while difficult, would also give an adversary access to information pertaining to every subscriber in the network. Recognizing this, HLRs are the best provisioned and physically protected elements within the cellular network.

3.2.3 Mobile Switching Center/Visiting Location Register

Mobile Switching Centers (MSCs) act as telephony switches and deliver circuit-switched traffic in a GSM network. Expressing their role so succinctly, however, fails to capture the magnitude of functions tasked to these devices. MSCs can act as gateways between a cellular network and *Public Switched Telephone Network* (PSTN). They connect the wireless portion of the network with core elements and have the most specific information about the location of users under their service. MSCs also facilitate mobility by assisting devices performing "handoffs" between base stations and assist in the billing process.

Managing such tasks requires more than simply switching. Because they are responsible for performing all of the above tasks, MSCs must be aware of context on a per-user basis. Such information can be retrieved from user profiles in the HLR; however, constant lookups in the HLR can be expensive for a number of reasons. Limited bandwidth network links (see Section 3.4), latency concerns and the impact of heightened load on the HLR all prevent such frequent lookups from occurring. To address these issues, temporary copies of user profiles are stored in a nearby database known as the *Visitor Location Register* (VLR). As shown in Table 3.1, the VLR contains many, but not all, of the same user profile data as the HLR. Most notably, the VLR does not have access to a user's K_i. This consideration is critical as phones can receive service from a network operated by a parties other than their provider.

The configuration between MSCs and VLRs varies from network to network. As shown in Figure 3.2, a single VLR may provide service to multiple MSCs. In other systems, the relationship between VLRs and MSCs is one-to-one, and such devices are co-located (and even referred to as MSC/VLRs or simply as MSCs). While the latter arrangement is more common in current networks, we distinguish between the functions of each wherever possible.

3.2.4 Base Station Subsystem

The link connecting wireless devices to a cellular network is provided by *Base Station Subsystems* (BSSs), which are composed of two components. *Base Transceiver Stations* (BTSs) are simply the radios used to transmit messages between mobile devices and the network. Most BTSs are composed of multiple (i.e., three) directional antennas that divide a each cell into smaller sectors (see Section 5.2.3 for more information). *Base Station Controllers* (BSCs) provide intelligence to the radios and are responsible for functions including scheduling and encryption. Deployment is often vendor specific - a single BSC can be combined with a single BTS, or a single BSC can service a large number of BTSs. In general, however, no distinction is made and the unit is generally collectively recognized as the BSS or base station.

Base stations are often arranged into groups of called *Location Areas* (LAs). Such groups often correspond to geographic regions. For instance, New

York City could potentially be divided into five LAs, each corresponding to one of five boroughs. [1] The advantage to dividing towers into such collections are numerous. Mobile devices not currently in a voice or data call with the network can move between towers within an LA without re-registering with the network. Only moves across LA boundaries cause inactive devices to notify the network of their new position. In so doing, signaling across the constrained SS7 and wired channels is greatly reduced.

Users actively using the network are required to perform a handoff for a number of reasons. As the number of users in a cell approaches capacity, the network may direct devices to the resources of a tower providing overlapping coverage. Similarly, if conditions on the wireless network degrade (e.g., increased noise), devices may also change towers. The third, and most common cause of handoffs, results from user mobility. When such an occasion arises, the transfer of device service between two base stations can occur in one of two ways. *Hard Handoffs* require a mobile device to drop its connection with its previous tower before attempting to tune into a neighboring cell. Such a transition should technically be instantaneous, but is often noticeable to users as seemingly unexplained gaps in conversation or prematurely terminated calls. *Soft Handoffs* allow a device to tune in to two or more base stations simultaneously, ensuring a more smooth transfer between cells. Logically, because soft handoffs allow the use of resources in multiple cells concurrently, they can reduce the overall capacity of the network. GSM networks implement hard handoffs between base stations; however, the majority of next generation systems will employ soft handoffs to improve overall quality.

3.3 Cellular Data Networks

3.3.1 Data Network Elements

The data communications system for GSM is called the *General Packet Radio Service* (GPRS). A simplified architecture is shown in Figure 3.3. Recognizing that many of the functions needed to provide cellular data service were already provided by the elements supporting voice in the network core, significant portions of the infrastructure are reused. In particular, signaling is done using SS7 and the HLR is used to perform authentication and store user profiles.

Supporting the new data networking capabilities also required the inclusion of a number of new core elements. In anticipation of high levels of data traffic, providers have deployed new higher bandwidth links within their networks. These links also connect two new network elements responsible for handling data – the *Gateway GPRS Support Node* (GGSN) and the *Serving GPRS Support Node* (SGSN). We examine these new elements in greater detail.

---

[1] Given its size and population density, such a division is too coarse. Accordingly, Location Areas in New York City are much smaller than this example.

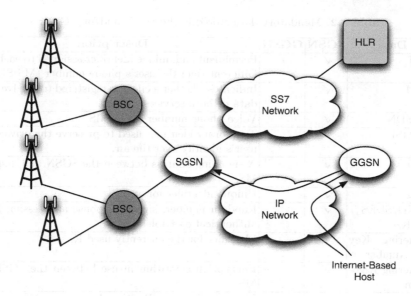

Fig. 3.3. The network architecture of GPRS/EDGE enabled cellular systems.

3.3.2 Gateway GPRS Support Node

Packets crossing the border between a cellular network and the Internet interact with a gateway between the two networks. This node, known as the *Gateway GPRS Support Node* (GGSN), is responsible for more than simply forwarding such packets to their ultimate destination. To provide support for multiple networking protocols, the GGSN can tunnel both IP and X.25 packets to a receiver. While the latter is rarely used, support is provided to ensure that older networks can support data services. GGSNs also provide support for operations more commonly associated with telecommunications networks. Granting and enforcing *Quality of Service* (QoS) markings on specific flows can be managed from the GGSN. The GGSN can also assist in the billing process by recording the amount of bandwidth used by each customer.

The most important function of the GGSN, however, is address and mobility management. As devices register with the network, the GGSN acts much like a DHCP server and assigns addresses. Both public (static) and private (dynamic) IP addresses are currently available from providers. After assigning an address, the GGSN then maintains a listing of the mobile device's current SGSN. Upon the arrival of incoming packets, the GGSN then performs a lookup on the targeted device, determines its SGSN and then tunnels the request.

Table 3.2. Mandatory data stored in the SGSN and/or GGSN.

Data	SGSN	GGSN	Description
IMSI	✓	✓	Permanent and unique identifier assigned to each user. Different than the user's phone number (MSISDN).
NAM	✓		Indicates whether a client is registered to receive voice, data or both services.
MSISDN	✓		Voice phone number for an MS.
P-TMSI	✓		Temporary identifier used to preserve the privacy of a user's identity over the air.
TLLI	✓		A signaling address between the SGSN and a specific MS.
IMEI	✓		Unique identifier for an MS.
RAND/SRES and K_C	✓		Random number, signed response and session key in authentication triplets.
Ciphering Key Seq. Number	✓		Identifier for the currently used K_C.
Ciphering Algorithm	✓		Encryption algorithm in use between the SGSN and MS.
RAI	✓		Identity of current Routing Area for an MS.
Cell Global Identification	✓		A concatenation of the LAI and the Cell Identity.
RA not allowed flag	✓		Applied to restrict service based on lack of roaming agreement or unsupported feature.
Roaming Restricted in the SGSN	✓		Roaming restricted in an SGSN because of an unsupported feature.
MNRG	✓	✓	MS not reachable because it is not GPRS attached.
MM State	✓	✓	The current mobility management state of an MS.
PDP Type	✓	✓	Indicates the protocol used by an MS for data communication (e.g., IP, X.25).
PDP Address	✓	✓	Lists the IP address of an MS.
NSAPI	✓	✓	Identifies a PDP context associated with an address.
SGSN address		✓	The IP address of the SGSN currently serving an MS.
QoS Negotiated	✓	✓	Notes the quality of service negotiated between an MS, its SGSN and the corresponding GGSN.
DRX Parameters	✓		Indicates that the MS is not constantly monitoring paging requests and that it should only be paged during certain times.
Classmark	✓		Specifies the classes of content (e.g., WAP, J2ME) an MS can support.

3.3.3 Serving GPRS Support Node

Much like MSCs, *Serving GPRS Support Nodes* (SGSNs) are responsible for more than simply moving packets toward their ultimate destination. With the assistance of a location register, the SGSN stores user profile information

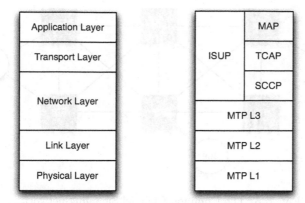

Fig. 3.4. The SS7 protocol stack with the Internet protocol stack as a reference for functionality.

locally. As is the case in MSCs, such profile information is valuable in assisting handoffs, performing authentication and in the billing process. Table 3.2, which is specified in standards documents [15], provides a list of the values stored by both GGSNs and SGSNs.

Because an HLR's knowledge of a user's current location is limited to their current SGSN, these nodes are responsible for tracking such information at a finer granularity. If a specific client is actively receiving data traffic, for instance, the SGSN records the cell or sector in which they are located. As such users move between cells, the SGSN is updated. To reduce the amount of signaling in the network, inactive but registered users (i.e., those whose devices are on but not currently exchanging packets with the network) generally do not alert the network of movement between cells or sectors. Like in the voice network, this is made possible by grouping multiple towers into sets. These *Routing Areas* (RAs) are typically smaller than their voice network Location Area counterparts.

Because many of the mobility management and authentication functions in GPRS are the same as those in pure GSM systems, many of these operations can be performed in parallel. For instance, when a device attempts to register with the voice portion of the network (see Section 3.6), the network can also register the device with the data elements automatically. To minimize the resources dedicate to locating a device, the MSC can defer the process of locating a user (known as paging) to that user's SGSN. Such optimizations are discussed in Chapter 6.

3.4 Signaling Network and Protocols

With an understanding of the core elements found in modern cellular networks, we now discuss the communications between them. We begin with an

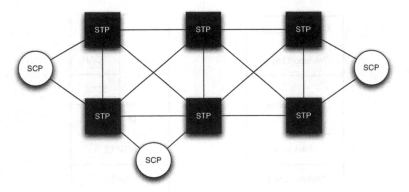

Fig. 3.5. The Common Channel Signaling network.

overview of the signaling network itself. Our focus the turns to the SS7 stack and the role played by each protocol layer in the network. Because we assume that most readers have some familiarity with the IP networking, we compare the functionality of each of the layers of the SS7 protocol stack with the Internet network model. Figure 3.4 provides a comparison of these protocol stacks.

3.4.1 Common Channel Signaling Network

The signaling messages exchanged between the switches, HLRs and VLRs are carried over the *Common Channel Signaling* (CCS) network and are part of the Signaling System No. 7 protocol suite. A simplified view of the CCS network is shown in Figure 3.5. The CCS network is built using special purpose highly redundant packet switches called *Signaling Transfer Points* (STPs). Any element that generates a signaling message (e.g., a HLR, VLR, or switch), is called a *Signaling Control Point* (SCP). All SCPs are connected to at least two STPs. STPs are connected in a quad arrangement. Using this configuration, no single failure in the CCS network will isolate a network element. Due to the cost of the STPs the CCS network is very tightly engineered.

3.4.2 Message Transfer Part

Forming the foundation of the SS7 protocol stack is the *Message Transfer Part* (MTP). MTP is tasked with the reliable delivery of signaling messages, including responding to link outages. In order to support this functionality, MTP is split into three distinct partitions.

Message Transfer Part Level 1 (MTP1) corresponds to the physical layer in the Internet model. All links are bidirectional and support bandwidths as high as 56 KBps in ANSI standard networks and 64 KBps elsewhere. Up to four physical links between two nodes can be combined to create an aggregate rate of 1.544 Mbps. In order to meet the real-time requirements of telephony, no link can operate at a bit rate of less than 4.8 kbps.

Message Transfer Part Level 2 (MTP2) provides link layer functionality for the SS7 protocol stack. Accordingly, communications between two directly connected network nodes are handled by MTP2. However, MTP2 provides far more functionality than simple point to point addressing. The first such functionality is reliable message delivery. This is in direct contrast to the Internet model, which uses end-to-end reliability services. Delivery guarantees are provided by the Go-Back-N algorithm, which relies upon negative acknowledgments to cause retransmission of packets within a window. Secondly, MTP strictly monitors the error rate of all links. Should the number of errors detected on the link surpass a threshold, MTP2 alerts higher level protocols and the link is shut down. The proper functioning of links is of paramount importance – filler packets are continuously transmitted on all links in the SS7 networks so that error detection can be constantly executed. Finally, MTP2 offers explicit flow control mechanisms. Should the congestion condition on a link exist for a number of seconds, the link is shut down. These functions are handled at such a low layer in order to maintain the real-time requirements of the network.

Many of the responsibilities traditionally assigned to Network layer protocols are provided by *Message Transfer Part Level 3* (MTP3). Accordingly, MTP3 is responsible for routing packets between sources and destinations. Whenever possible, each STP will attempt to balance traffic sent across each link. Like the Internet model, each packet may therefore take slightly different paths through the network. Messages that must be kept strictly in sequence, however, can be flagged to use the same physical link. MTP3 also responds to link outages reported by MTP2. Whether from from processor failure, high link errors or congestion, MTP3 will reconfigure routes around unavailable neighbors to ensure that traffic is delivered. The combination of redundant links and the ability to react quickly to network failure allow such networks to maintain their extremely high levels of availability.

3.4.3 Signaling Connection Control Part

The routing functionality provided MTP3 is somewhat limited. The *Signaling Connection Control Part* (SCCP) addresses these issues by providing the remaining functions common to Network layer protocols. Whereas MTP3 messages can only address nodes in the network, SCCP allows specific functions to become the destination of a request. For instance, support for special global numbers, such as 800 numbers, are supported by SCCP. Requests can be delivered using one of five classes of service. Classes 0 and 1 are connectionless and differ only by the ability to request that all packets be sent on the same physical link in the case of the latter. Classes 2 and 3 are both connection-oriented and require that all packets be delivered over the same links. They differ, however, in that Class 3 SCCP messages provide flow control. Class 4 messages are the same as Class 3, but allows for messages that can not be properly reassembled to be retransmitted.

In conjunction with the three levels of MTP, SCCP forms what is referred to as the *Network Services Part* (NSP).

3.4.4 Transaction Capabilities Application Part

For services control, including mobility management, a transaction-oriented protocol called the *Transactions Capabilities Application Part* (TCAP) is used. TCAP provides a framework through which nodes throughout the network can request the execution of remote procedures. For instance, *Intelligent Network* (IN) functions such as toll free calling and automatic call blocking are invoked with TCAP messages. TCAP messages also provide transaction identifiers, which are functionally similar to port numbers in transport layer protocols.

3.4.5 Mobile Application Part

The majority of the network-supported procedures discussed in this book use the *Mobile Application Part* (MAP). MAP provides application layer functionality to SS7 networks. Services visible to the user, including call handling, text messaging and location-based services are all carried by MAP messages. Less visible services, such as mobility management (both within and outside their home network), service profile downloads between HLRs and VLRs, and authentication procedures are all conducted using MAP.

Because MAP messages contain so much critical information, they must be protected. We briefly discuss MAPsec in Section 3.7 and its associated security weaknesses in Chapter 4.

3.4.6 ISDN User Part

For connection control, the *Integrated Services Digital Network* (ISDN) User Part (ISUP) is used. ISUP carries information so that calls may be routed and resources reserved along the path. It is used for both fixed and mobile networks. In fixed networks, routing is done based on the dialed number. In mobile networks, the first portion of the connection is established using the dialed number; from the gateway MSC to the serving MSC, the call is routed based on the temporary routing number. ISUP messages are routing hop-by-hop through each switch through which the connect will pass.

3.5 Wireless Network

In the following subsections we discuss various facets of the wireless portion of the network including access techniques, frequency issues, voice coding, and provide a brief summary of procedures.

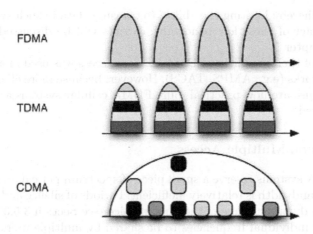

Fig. 3.6. Representations of the three main methods of spectrum access: FDMA, TDMA and CDMA.

3.5.1 Wireless Access Techniques

Dividing wireless spectrum into a medium capable of supporting many users can be achieved through a number of approaches. While many other methods for wireless access exist, the frequency-, time- and code-division multiple access represent the three technologies currently use by cellular telecommunications networks. Each of these general classes has a direct impact on voice quality, interference and the maximum number of users supportable in a cell. Figure 3.6 offers a comparison of these three methods.

Frequency-Division Multiple Access

Frequency-Division Multiple Access (FDMA) is the most basic means of providing concurrent wireless access to multiple parties. Users in an FDMA system each receive exclusive access to independent frequencies, which are referred to as *carriers*. Such separation simplifies a number of systems issues. For instance, hosts do not need to be synchronized in time with each other. Additionally, hardware support is vastly simplified as devices only need to be able to tune to specific frequencies.

For their simplicity, FDMA systems suffer from a number of notable disadvantages. First, in order to prevent two frequencies from interfering, calls in a FDMA must be separated by guard bands – unused spectrum in which interference between two frequencies is likely to be high. The size of guard bands is highly dependent upon the carrier bandwidth allocated in the system. For instance, AMPS used 30 kHz carriers with kHz guard bands. The absence of such buffers could significantly improve capacity of such systems. Moreover, as the number of users in the system increases, so too does the amount of interference. Pure FDMA systems also suffer from a fixed, relatively low bit rate per carrier, thereby limiting the ability to transmit data in such systems. The security impact of these low bandwidth carriers will be discussed in greater detail in Chapter 5.

Because of their simplicity, FDMA wireless access was used in analog (1G) cellular networks (e.g., AMPS, TACS). However, because more efficient means of spectrum use are now practical, pure FDMA cellular systems are no longer being deployed.

Time-Division Multiple Access

While FDMA systems reserve a small piece of spectrum per caller, the utilization of this bandwidth is relatively inefficient. Periods of silence and short-term limits on the dynamic range of the human voice (see Section 3.5.3) create the potential for individual frequencies to be shared by multiple users. Recognizing this, *Time-Division Multiple Access* (TDMA) systems provide service to users by partitioning a frequency into evenly sized timeslots. Devices listen to a single timeslot, each of which are serviced in a round-robin fashion. In GSM, for instance, each frequency on the air interface is divided into eight timeslots, each of which are serviced every 4.615 msec. As the device samples its assigned timeslot across multiple iterations, a virtual channel is created.

TDMA systems offer a number of advantages over their FDMA counterparts. Because multiple users can share a frequency band, the number of concurrently supportable by such a system is significantly increased. Moreover, the guard bands need to protect users in FDMA systems are no longer required between channels[2], although they do require guard times. Devices listening to a single timeslot, as opposed to constantly monitoring a frequency, also dramatically increase the lifetime of their batteries. Finally, by allowing mobile phones to potentially listen to multiple timeslots, TDMA systems also allow flexible bit-rates for data communications.

These improvements over FDMA come at the cost of complexity. Because access to wireless resources is based on time-division, all devices in the network must be tightly time synchronized. To protect against clock drift, each timeslot must be buffered between guard-time so as to reduce the probability that two devices will accidentally overhear each other. Devices must also frequently resynchronize with the network in order to maintain their ability to operate between the guard-time buffers. Finally, because multiple devices are transmitting on the same frequency, multipath distortion (i.e., reflections of signal received later than the intended timeslot) can significantly impact call quality.

While these costs are significant, TDMA cellular networks far outperform FDMA systems. Examples of deployed networks relying on this technology

---

[2] In practice, guard bands are still used in real TDMA networks such as GSM as networks use TDMA over multiple frequencies to increase the number of supportable users.

include IS-136 and GSM, the most widely deployed cellular networking technology in the world [79].

Code-Division Multiple Access

Code-Division Multiple Access (CDMA) systems avoid the issue of separating users by time and space by allowing them to transmit simultaneously on the same frequency. To achieve this, each user in a cell receives a unique code (i.e., mask) to spread the spectrum they transmit in to each bit of their data. The size of this code is many times larger than each bit.

Wireless access via CDMA has a number of advantages over the two previously discussed methods. The process of coding transmission not only allows users to a share frequency range, but also makes na ive of confidentiality for the system. Unlike FDMA and TDMA systems in which an adversary can simply scan frequencies or timeslots to intercept traffic, locating a specific signal from within the combined traffic of the network is computationally infeasible as the chip rate becomes large without knowledge of a specific code. However, most codes are available as part of the specification, thereby reducing the search space of an attacker. The additive nature of the coding also places no theoretical limit on the number of users that can be supported in a single area; rather, the number of users to be supported can be increased at the expense of the quality of service received. Moreover, the spreading of signal across a wide band of frequencies reduces the impact of multipath distortion and provides improved quality for voice.

Systems using CDMA face a number of challenges. Because of the additive nature of the coding, the network must keep strict control over the transmission power used by each of the nodes in a cell. As devices move towards and away from the tower and pass behind occlusions, the effort needed to coordinate power control becomes significant. Devices can also potentially self-jam if the pseudo-noise sequences used to spread their signal across the spectrum are not exactly orthogonal.

In spite of these difficulties, CDMA schemes represent the most advanced wireless access systems in the world. Originally used by the military because of their inherent confidentiality and robustness to jamming, CDMA systems are increasingly being used in the civilian arena. While the use of CDMA radios is largely limited to cellular networks in the United States (e.g., IS-95), all major third generation networks will use CDMA-based radios as their wireless access method.

3.5.2 Frequency Issues

Frequency Assignment

In spite of being the most widely deployed cellular networking technology, a GSM-capable mobile device may not be able to interact with every GSM network it encounters. Even in the presence of nearly universal roaming agreements, one issue still impedes access to telephony services through any GSM network on the globe – frequency assignment. Because each nation is able to regulate how the wireless spectrum is divided and used within their borders, consistent use of spectrum across the world does not exist.

In response, GSM systems exist in one of a number of possible frequency bands. The first networks, deployed largely in Europe, operated within the 900 MHz band and are referred to as GSM-900. These systems, which offer a total of 124 bidirectional 200 kHz carriers, now represent the vast majority of deployed GSM networks in the world, and are deployed on every inhabited continent. In response to rising demand on these networks, most GSM-900 systems now also include an additional 50 carriers and are referred to as Extended-GSM networks (EGSM). Because this portion of the spectrum was already dedicated for other purposes in many locations, other GSM systems transmit at twice the original frequency, or 1800 MHz, and offer up to 374 carriers. Such networks, known as GSM-1800, can be found throughout the United Kingdom, Brazil and parts of Southeast Asia [80].

Similar problems of spectrum allocation exist in the Americas. Because the 900 MHz frequency range used in GSM-900 systems was already allocated to other systems (e.g., IS-54), new spectrum had to be dedicated to support GSM. In less densely populated areas, providers deployed GSM-850. Largely similar to GSM-900 (i.e., supports up to 123 carriers), these networks take advantage of these lower frequency waves to expand their coverage areas. Because higher frequency transmissions allow for increased capacity (up to 298 carriers), GSM-1900 has been deployed in larger metropolitan areas. Such deployment strategies are not compulsory, but generally guide the specific technology deployed when creating new coverage areas.

With all of these possibilities, a logical question arises: Given a mobile device with a single radio, in which frequency band should that device listen in order to receive uninterrupted service? In the ideal case, a provider's network would offer widespread coverage using a single band. In reality, however, neither of these conditions holds. Mobile users may require the use of other networks operating in a different frequency band to maintain connectivity. This case is especially common as users cross national borders. Moreover, a single provider may deploy base stations operating in different frequency bands throughout their network. Accordingly, devices must be able to tune into multiple frequencies in order to ensure service. The majority of modern mobile devices therefore come with so-called *tri-band* and *quad-band* capabilities, which allow them to operate in the presence of most (three) and all GSM frequency bands, respectively.

Frequency Reuse

In spite of the seemingly large wireless capacity available to GSM networks, no single cell has access to the full complement of carriers described above. For

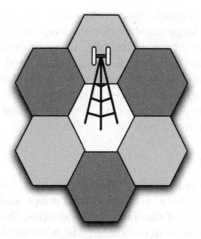

Fig. 3.7. A series of cells in a network with a frequency reuse factor, F_u, of three. Note that no cell borders another cell operating on the same frequency.

instance, if multiple providers offer service to a single geographic area, the spectrum must be divided between them. Moreover, no two bordering cells can use the same carriers, because calls occurring on the same carriers in two neighboring cells will create significant *co-channel interference*. Accordingly, spectrum reuse across cells must be carefully planned.

We use Figure 3.7 and a GSM-900 network to step through a simple example. Accordingly, a total of 124 carriers will be available for all GSM activity in this region. As is done in many real networks are planned, cells are assumed to be hexagonal in shape. For the purposes of this example, we assume that two providers offer competing service within this geographic region. Assuming equal division of resources between the two providers, this immediately halves the number of available carriers. In order to prevent calls in two cells from interfering, a frequency reuse factor, F_u, of three is set. Accordingly, the number of carriers that any one cell can use is further divided by F_u. If cells are further divided into sectors, the number of carriers is again divided by three. The maximum number of TDMA channels that can be provided in each sector of such a network is therefore:

$$Channels = \lfloor \frac{124 \text{ carriers}}{2 \text{ providers}} \times \frac{1}{3(F_u)} \times \frac{1 \text{ cell}}{3 \text{ sectors}} \rfloor \times \frac{8 \text{ channels}}{1 \text{ carrier}}$$
$$= 48 \text{ channels/sector/provider}$$

Given such a setup, it may be possible for a provider to support as many as 46 concurrent voice and data calls in an area (the other two channels would be used for network signaling). The implications of such an arrangement are, in many ways, more complex. Some cells cover an area of up to 10 square miles, meaning that a large number of users may be forced to compete for a relatively small number of total channels. In more densely populated areas, much smaller micro- and pico-cells may instead be used to combat this problem. However, the relationship between cell/sector size and F_u is inversely proportional. Accordingly, the number of cells that must be between two cells using the same frequency must increase. Network planning must therefore be done in an extremely careful fashion.

Frequency Hopping

While carefully planning frequency reuse throughout a coverage area can significantly reduce interference, GSM networks adopt additional techniques in order to lessen the impact of unrelated transmissions. Because frequency reuse generally protects devices from each other, the most significant source of interference is often a device's own signals. As mentioned in Section 3.5.1, signals reflecting off of nearby objects (e.g., buildings) can considerably degrade the quality of a connection. Much like speaking loudly in a room without sound dampening materials, unaccounted-for multipath distortion can literally make coherent communication impossible.

GSM networks deal with multipath distortion by regularly changing the frequency used within a cell. This technique, known as *frequency hopping*, allows devices simply to tune into a new frequency and timeslot. Instead of receiving signals that may be consistently in the opposite phase of the transmissions sent by the tower, this technique randomizes the effects of interference. Because random noise can easily be removed using error correcting codes, the overall quality of calls in the network is drastically improved. Note that this frequency hopping occurs at a much flower rate than spread spectrum systems that use frequency hopping explicitly (e.g., Bluetooth).

Frequency hopping in GSM can operate under one of two modes – cyclic and pseudorandom [22, 18]. In order to determine the mode used in a sector, devices simply listen for the broadcast of the *Hopping Sequence Number* (HSN) on the control channels. If HSN is set to zero, devices simply use the next highest numbered carrier above their current position at each frequency change. After reaching the highest available carrier, devices simply wrap around to their provider's lowest available carrier. If the HSN is set to a number between 1 and 63, devices change carriers according to tables of pseudo-randomly generated sequences. While cyclic frequency hopping is easier to implement, the use of pseudo-random sequences better randomizes the multipath distortion observed by mobile devices.

Future Frequency Management Issues

The most critical problem facing cellular providers in the future, according to most members of the industry, is spectrum allocation. While current narrowband (200 kHz/carrier) GSM networks deliver voice and data services, higher bandwidth services and improved connection to larger IP networks (i.e., the Internet) will only be possible through the allocation of new spectrum. Unfortunately, procuring additional spectrum for so-called wide-band services is a timely and expensive process. Most large portions of the usable spectrum have already been allocated. Accordingly, buyers must often wait for technology that previously had exclusive access to a frequency band to become obsolete or unused. Because such events are fairly infrequent, competition for new spectrum is often intense. Wireless providers have, in the past, proposed bids for tens of billions of dollars for access to these new bands.

Spectrum allocation will continue to be a major issue facing all wireless providers in the foreseeable future. At the time of this writing, the *Ultra-High Frequency* (UHF) portion of the spectrum once used for analog television (the 700 MHz band) has only recently been divided by public auction. Unlike previous auctions, however, a number of non-traditional parties expressed interest in acquiring a portion of this band. Google, for instance, proposed an initial offer of US$4.6 Billion [67]. Because it is unlikely that another large portion of the wireless spectrum will become available again during the next decade, bidding grew to over $19 Billion in total [70]. The implications of this auction will take time to become obvious.

3.5.3 Voice Encoding

Modern cellular networks provide high-quality voice communications via digital encoding. Until the mid 1990's, however, only analog service was available. Analog phone systems suffer from a number of significant limitations. As mentioned in Section 3.1, systems such as AMPS operate by transmitting each call on distinct frequencies. The maximum number of users supported in each cell is therefore directly dependent upon wireless spectrum allocation – an expensive and infrequently conducted process. Because noise in analog signals is added at each hop along its traversal between source and destination, the quality of voice telephony is such systems was low. This inability to transmit high-fidelity signals was one of the chief limiting factors in using encryption in early mobile phone systems.

Digital cellular systems offer significant improvements in spectrum efficiency, bandwidth and voice quality. Whether in a TDMA (e.g., IS-136, GSM) or CDMA (e.g., IS-95) system, modern systems no longer require a single frequency per user in an area. Instead, devices in these systems sample, digitize and compress speech. While we focus on the specific mechanisms available to GSM networks, similar techniques are used across all systems.

Analog signals are encoded digitally through *Pulse Code Modulation* (PCM). Instead of capturing the entire analog signal itself, PCM uses regular sampling and records a binary representation of the magnitude of the sound wave. Each sample is encoded as an integer, and a ceiling function is used to remove ambiguity. The G.711 encoder, which takes either 14-bit or 13-bit signed integers depending on the compression algorithm applied (μ-law

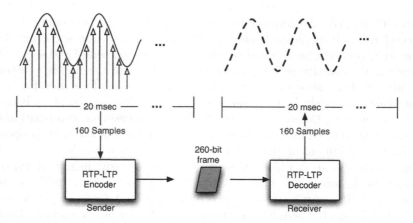

Fig. 3.8. A high level overview of voice encoding. Voice is sampled (white arrows) at a rate of 8,000 times per second (8 kHz) using PCM. Groups of 160 samples (20 msec) are then sent to the RPE-LTP encoder, which generates a 260 bit frame. When this frame is delivered to the receiving client, the reverse process occurs and the voice signals are reconstructed.

and A-law, respectively), then converts each of the inputs into 8-bit samples [93]. At a sampling rate of 8,000 times per second (8 kHz), the resulting voice stream is encoded at 64 kbps. As a comparison, CD quality audio is typically recorded at 1411.2 kbps [88].

While music requires a high bitrate encoding to capture its dynamic and potentially complex nature, because of physical limitations governing the speed in which the mouth can meaningfully change sounds, much of the information included in the 64 kbps stream is redundant. Accordingly, speech encoding can be made more efficient by removing unneeded samples. To achieve these ends, phones apply the Regular Pulse Excitation - Long Term Prediction (RPE-LTP) algorithm, which reduces the average bit rate of the stream to 13 kbps [8, 10]. RPE-LTP takes as input either the unmodified A- or μ-law code or can convert the above 8-bit data to the 13-bit uniform PCM format [94]. The encoder then takes batches of 160 samples (20 msec) and outputs 260-bit encoded blocks. When received by the phone at the other end of a connection, each 260-bit block are used to reconstruct the 160 speech samples. This process is summarized in Figure 3.8.

Reducing the bandwidth required to transmit voice between two parties not only improves spectrum utilization, but also saves power. As mobile phones have traditionally been highly resource constrained, such an improvement significantly improves the lifetime of such devices. Applying additional context-specific information can provide further power savings. For instance, during an average phone call, each user is likely to speak for approximately 50% of the conversation. Accordingly, there is no need for a device to transmit when its user is silent. *Discontinuous Transmission* (DTX) mode addresses this condition by allowing a device's transmitter to be turned off when a user is not producing "useful" information [7]. In order to determine whether or not a user is producing useful information, DTX relies upon *Voice Activity Detection* (VAD) [26]. VAD analyzes the 20 msec frames generated by the RPE-LTP algorithm to determine whether or not speech is present. If only background noise is detected, the transmitting phone does not send a frame.

While saving a notable amount of power, pure DTX mode is often criticized for adding a decidedly mechanical characteristic to a conversation. Much like two individuals communicating via walkie-talkies, the detection of silence by VAD often makes a voice seem choppy and unnatural given the small detection window. The receiving side is also left listening to silence, which is also frequently confused with call disconnection. These problems are addressed through the addition of "comfort noise" [6]. When VAD determines that voice signals are no longer being sent, the phone transmits a final frame containing a *Silence Descriptor* (SID). This frame includes information to assist the receiving side to generate noise similar to that present on the transmitting side during periods of silence.

There are a number of reasons that individual frames of encoded voice are not received by a destination device. The air interface is inherently noisy and, while error correcting encoding can improve proper reconstruction, some frames can simply not be recovered. The network may also purposefully drop packets in a process known as frame stealing. Frame stealing allows a provider to conduct signaling to users already engaged in a call in-band. For instance, if the user needs to be alerted of an incoming call-waiting request, the network drops a frame of the current conversation to notify the user. For single frames dropped due to noise or for non-disruptive signaling requests (i.e., not call-waiting), devices can either repeat the previous frame or extrapolate the missing values from previous successful frames [9]. The loss of multiple frames is handled by temporarily muting the call.

These techniques allow for wireless providers to offer high-quality voice communications at greatly reduced costs when compared to previous analog systems. Digital encoding reduces the average bandwidth needed to transmit voice by a factor of four over analog methods. In combination with techniques such as DTX, these systems can provide power-efficient yet natural sounding voice between two parties.

3.5.4 Summary of Procedures

To complete registration, location update or call procedures over the air interface, elaborate signaling exchanges are performed over well structured control channels. The details of these control channels are discussed in later chapters. Here we discuss one subtle, but significant service provided on the air interface that provides some measure of privacy. We present it here because this eases the understanding of the discussion in latter sections of this chapter.

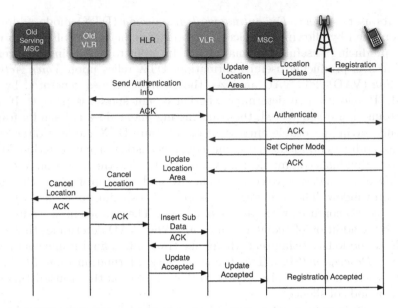

Fig. 3.9. The message flow for a mobile device registration.

To protect the privacy of a mobile device, during each registration and location update, the mobile device is given a pseudonym called a *Temporary Mobile Subscriber Identifier* (TMSI) that is sent over an encrypted channel. This TMSI is the identifier used by the mobile device when communicating over the air. In this way, an eavesdropper cannot track the location of a device. The TMSI used as the index into the subscriber records in the access portion of the network, i.e., by the VLRs and MSCs.

3.6 Registration and Call Setup Procedures

We now explain the operation of the mobile network through an example. Please refer to Figures 3.9 and 3.10 during the following discussion.

At a high level, the user registration with the network occurs as follows: The registration message (or location update message), is sent to the serving MSC/VLR. If the device has already registered previously, it uses its TMSI as its identifier. If the MSC/VLR do not have a record for the mobile device, the message is routed to the HLR of the user based on its mobile telephone number. After authentication procedures are performed, the details of which are discussed in Section 3.8, the HLR enters the current VLR serving the mobile device into its database. A copy of the user's service profile is then sent from the HLR to the VLR. At this time, the HLR points to the VLR, and the MSC/VLR has the ability to provide services to the mobile device.

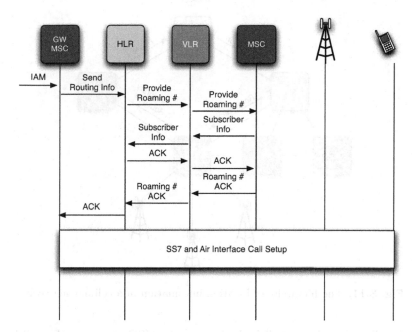

Fig. 3.10. The message flow for call setup to a mobile phone.

When a mobile device is powered on, or if it moves, it must register with the network using the procedures described above so that it can be located if a call for it is placed. While the HLR records the MSC/VLR currently serving the user, it is not aware of a user's current LA. Location updates to the HLR are only made when a mobile device's MSC/VLR changes or periodically to alert the network that it is still alive. A mobile device's serving MSC/VLR stores its current LA. A summary of the hierarchy of location information is shown in Figure 3.11.

Having registered with the network, a mobile device can then receive incoming voice calls. Such calls can originate from mobile devices within and outside a provider's network, from the PSTN or an external data network such as the Internet. Regardless, call setup begins by the transmission of an *Initial Address Message* (IAM). The gateway MSC receiving this message determines the HLR corresponding to the targeted phone number and then sends a request for that device's current location. Upon receiving this request, the HLR performs a lookup on the device and then queries the MSC/VLR listed as currently serving the device. If the MSC/VLR responds with the correct user profile information and the HLR acknowledges receiving this information, the MSC/VLR forwards a temporary local phone number by which a targeted device can be addressed. Having received a temporary routing address known as the *Mobile Station Routing Number* (MSRN), which lasts only as long as it

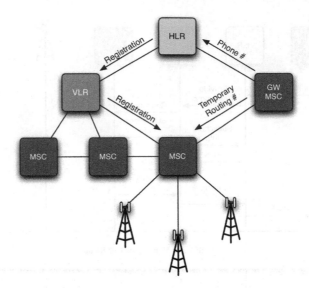

Fig. 3.11. The hierarchy of location information in a cellular network.

takes for the call to be established, the gateway MSC can route the call itself toward the serving MSC/VLR and ultimately the user. Chapter 5 provides the remaining details of how calls are delivered between the MSC/VLR and the mobile device.

Those readers familiar with Mobile IPv6 [101] will notice a number of high-level similarities between it and the SS7 network. HLR's, for instance, provide forwarding service much like a *Home Agent* (HA). The MSC/VLR implement much of the functionality associated with a *Foreign Agent* (FA). While the comparison is not strictly one-to-one, this abstraction may be helpful to readers.

3.7 Core Network Security

Recently, efforts to provide *Network Domain Security* (NDS) have been made to secure the core of the mobile telecommunication network. The aim of these efforts is to provide authentication of signaling messages between network nodes and networks, and to guarantee message integrity. Message confidentially can also be provided. The instantiation of NDS is a protocol targeted at protecting MAP called MAPsec [20, 24]. Thus, security is provided at the application layer.

MAPsec allows security associations to be established internally between network nodes and, more commonly, between networks. Shared cryptographic keys may be distributed manually or automatically using protocols such as IKE [84]. When activated, MAPsec can be applied to all or only a subset of

Table 3.3. MAPsec Protection Levels

Level	Invoke	Result	Error
1	PM1 (Integ.)	PM0 (No Protection)	PM0 (No Protection)
2	PM1 (Integ.)	PM1 (Integ.)	PM0 (No Protection)
3	PM1 (Integ.)	PM2 (Integ. + Conf.)	PM0 (No Protection)
4	(Integ. + Conf.)	PM1 (Integ.)	PM0 (No Protection)
5	(Integ. + Conf.)	PM2 (Integ. + Conf.)	PM0 (No Protection)
6	(Integ. + Conf.)	PM0 (No Protection)	PM0 (No Protection)

messages passing through the network. When MAPsec is used it may provide integrity only or encryption and integrity. Integrity is ensured by generating a CBC MAC using AES over the security header. Encryption is provided using AES counter mode.

MAPsec provides six levels of protection, known as *Protection Modes* (PMs) as shown in Table 3.3. The PM applied to a particular message of set of messages depends on the information communicated. For example, PM3 is suggested for use on messages related to authentication. The invocation of authentication does not contain any secret information, but the reply from the HLR includes the various keys used for encryption and integrity, and must therefore be kept confidential. Handover requests use PM4 because their invocation contains the TMSI. This must be kept confidential so an eavesdropper on the signaling network cannot correlate the mobility of a user; however, only the integrity of the response is protected.

MAPsec is not widely available. In fact, at a panel on telecommunications security at the 2007 USENIX Security Symposium, it was revealed that only a single deployment of MAPsec has ever been fielded. MAPsec's widespread incorporation into live networks was cut short by the substantial degradation it imposed on network performance. Accordingly, many vendor products simply do not include MAPsec capabilities and no known network current runs the protocol [47]. Performance issues aside, MAPsec can assist in combating some message insertion and modifications. However, it will not protect against propagation of attacks if they are launched from a legitimate network or node and a series of other attacks [110].

3.8 Air Interface Security

On the air interface of GSM, there are three main algorithms. The A3 algorithm is used for authentication, A8 for generating a cipher key, and A5 for ciphering data. All security operations are based on a 128 bit key, K_i, shared between the mobile device (actually, the SIM card in the mobile device) and the HLR.

A flow highlighting the authentication procedures is shown in Figure 3.12. When a mobile device first registers with a network, the VLR retrieves a set

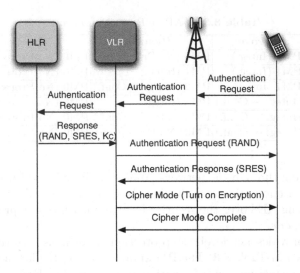

Fig. 3.12. The challenge/response authentication protocol for GSM.

of five triplets from the HLR: RAND, SRES, and K_c. RAND is a random
value used by the VLR to challenge the mobile device. SRES is the expected
response to the challenge. K_c is the cipher key to be used for communication.
When the VLR receives the set of triplets, it challenges the mobile device
with RAND. Using the A3 algorithm with K_i and RAND as input, the mobile
device computes and returns a 32-bit SRES to the VLR which compares it
to the expected value. If it matches, the mobile device is authenticated. In
essence, the HLR authenticates the mobile device. The mobile device uses the
A8 algorithm with K_i and RAND as input to generate the 64-bit cipher key,
K_c used to protect subsequent communication.

The base GSM security solution has many weaknesses. First, the algorithms are supposed to be secret, but in fact have been found to be typically
COMP128. As we will discuss in Chapter 4, COMP128 can be broken using
a chosen challenge attack. Second, while the cipher key is specified as 64 bits,
it is typically 54 bits padded with zeros and can be broken with a brute force
attack. Third, the mobile device does not authenticate the network. This has
led to false base station attacks in which an adversary can perform chosen
challenge attacks and learn the identity of mobile devices by sending it messages. Finally, the use of encryption in these systems was terminated at the
base station. Because wireless backhaul (e.g., microwave links) is often used to
connect base stations to central offices, eavesdroppers could learn challenges
and responses, mobile device identifiers, and most critically, cryptographic
keys.

Many of these issues were address with the introduction of UMTS. The
procedures in terms of message flows for UMTS are similar to those of GSM,
but different information is carried in the messages. UMTS uses five algo-

rithms, F1-F5. The algorithms use a random number, RAND, some local material, a sequence number and a key, K, shared with the mobile, as input at the HLR. F1 outputs a MAC, F2 outputs a signed response (XRES), F3 outputs a cipher key (CK), F4 outputs an integrity key (IK) and F5 outputs an authentication key (AK). The sequence number, AK, local material and MAC are used to generate an authentication token, AUTN. Upon registration, the HLR sends the VLR a set of 5-tuples: RAND, XRES, CK, IK, and AUTN.

The mobile device is sent RAND and AUTN and has local copies of the local material and K. Using these items it can compute XRES, MAC, CK, IK, and AUTN. The AUTN is an authentication token for the network. If the AUTN computed by the device matches the AUTN it received, the device has authenticated the network. If so, it returns the XRES to the VLR for comparison. If the XRES supplied by the mobile device matches the XRES provided by the HLR, the network has authenticated the mobile device. In this way, mutual authentication is performed. CK is used by the mobile device to encrypt all communications. IK is used by the network to sign signaling messages. It is used because the network may command the mobile device to send information in the clear, i.e., disable ciphering. To prevent false base stations from performing this operation, signaling messages are signed with IK.

UMTS uses the public KASUMI algorithm as the basis of its algorithms. Also, encryption is carried back into the wired network to prevent eavesdropping. Combined, these improvements overcome most of the limitations of GSM air interface security from the perspective of stealing service and cloning.

3.9 Summary

In this chapter, we presented an overview of the architecture of a GSM network. We began by offering a historical perspective and providing an intuition behind some of the design decisions made in currently deployed networks. For instance, by understanding the weaknesses of analog cellular systems such as AMPS, it is possible to see why security appeared to be a largely "solved" problem in digital networks from the provider perspective. We then explored the nodes, protocols and physical connections needed to support both voice and data services in GSM networks. Issues ranging from the details of a user's profile and device registration to spectrum allocation offered insight into the many complex technical and political challenges facing real systems. We concluded by discussing the mechanisms used to provide security for both the core and wireless portions of these networks.

Our scope thus far has been intentionally broad. While the information covered in this chapter certainly covered some topics in depth, it is simply not possible to cover every aspect of these complex systems in a single book. However, readers with a good grasp of the information in this chapter will be well equipped to begin tackling the security issues facing current and next generation networks. The vulnerabilities discussed throughout the remainder of this book can, in fact, are all discoverable using this material. We encourage readers with curiosity in one of the many aspects of the network that we have not discussed in explicit detail to begin their own research in the standards documents.

Part II

Vulnerability Analysis

4

Vulnerabilities in the Telephony

The physical and logical isolation of cellular networks from other systems has long provided many of the advantages of so called "air-gap" security. Even still, these networks have historically exhibited significant security vulnerabilities. In this chapter, we explore many of the most critical of such weaknesses. Our examination ranges from the collapse of proprietary cryptographic algorithms and the lack of authenticated messages between elements in the network core to a growing pool of smart phone-based malware. In combination with the attacks discussed in the coming chapters, the information in this chapter can help the reader understand the current state of security in cellular networks.

4.1 Weak Cryptographic Algorithms

For much of the history of cryptography, ensuring that a cipher remained secret was an integral part of protecting the confidentiality of data. However, the passage of time has repeatedly demonstrated that secret algorithms as simple as the Caesar Cipher to the complex Content Scramble System (CSS) used to protect DVDs frequently contain fatal weaknesses. Starting around the turn of the twentieth century, however, a movement toward the creation of strong, publicly vetted algorithms arose. Spurred by Kerckhoff's principle, which states that strong algorithms must assume that adversaries possess complete knowledge of the system, the majority of modern cryptography is instead based around the idea that secrecy lies in the key and not the algorithm.

While history provides us with countless examples of proprietary cryptographic algorithms failing once examined by adversaries, cellular providers and equipment manufacturers have long resisted analysis of the algorithms used to provide authentication and confidentiality in their networks. We offer a brief overview of how the most critical current and next-generation algorithms have been broken through cryptanalysis.

From the perspective of the network, the most important function of cryptography is the ability to vet users as they attempt to login to a network. Unique identification allows a provider to associate the use of specific services with a specific account, thereby providing a means of accurate, unforgeable billing. In GSM networks, this functionality is embodied generically as A3/A8, which is specifically implemented by variants of the COMP128 algorithm. Specifically, the A3 algorithm is tasked with authenticating a user with the network using a 128-bit key K_i (See Chapter 3). The A8 algorithm creates a 64-bit session key K_c, which consists of the last 54-bits generated by the COMP128 algorithm and 10 zeros appended to the end, for communication with the network. While the use of COMP128 for authentication was believed to be strong (given the key length), a number of attacks have been demonstrated by the academic community. For instance, Goldberg et al [75] noted that the secret key K_i could be recovered by querying a GSM SIM card approximately 2^{19} times, which can take between six and eight hours to accomplish. Soon after this work was published, the code for COMP128 was leaked and published on multiple sites on the Internet. Rao et al [144] used this information later to dramatically improve the performance of attacks against COMP128, creating a method through which K_i could be recovered in under one minute. Accordingly, the COMP128 is widely viewed, even by the industry, as a vulnerable algorithm.

A number of mitigations have been proposed to protect against the weakness of COMP128. For example, many smart card developers limited the functional lifetimes of their SIM cards to under 2^{16} operations. While this mechanism certainly prevents the original attack by Goldberg et al, it does not prevent more modern attacks such as the work by Rao et al. More critically, it allows malicious code to potentially deny a legitimate user the ability to use their phone (See Chapter 5). Most networks, however, now rely on modified versions of the COMP128 algorithm, known as COMP128-2 and COMP128-3. While the GSM trade organization, GSM World, actively supports the adoption of one of these algorithms [81], it is unclear how many networks have fully upgraded beyond the original COMP128 algorithm. Specifically, full substitution of A3/A8 algorithms requires that all SIM devices are replaced. Because the details of these new algorithms remain private[1], little is known of their strength.

From the perspective of the user, the most important security feature provided by the network is the confidentiality of conversations. Unlike the Internet, the vast majority of people believe that their communications via cellular networks can not be intercepted by third parties. The network, in fact, does provide encryption for voice calls between the user's phone and the base station. In GSM networks, this algorithm is known generically as A5 and comes in a number of variants. A5/1, for instance, is used through-

---

[1] Publicly, it is claimed the COMP128-2 and COMP128-3 fix the problems of COMP128, with COMP128-3 addressing the appended zeros in K_c.

out the United States and Europe. Due to the political environment at the time of their development, the purposefully weakened A5/2 algorithm was developed for export to other parts of the world. Like A3/A8 before them, however, both such algorithms were found to be critically flawed when examined by external cryptographers. Golic [77] published the first cryptanalysis of the algorithm believed to be A5/1 and discovered that the key could be recovered in approximately 2^{40} operations. Biryukov et al [43] developed the first such attack in 2000, in which they demonstrated the ability to recover an A5/1 key (K_c) by processing the first two minutes of a conversation using a standard desktop PC with 128MB or RAM and two 73 GB hard drives. This attack was able to successfully able to recover the key in under one second. Biham and Dunkelman successfully reduced the complexity of the attack and decreased the storage to execute it to 38 GB [41]. Barkan et al [148] then developed an attack requiring no preprocessing and only a short sample of known text. Petrovic et al [138] instead examined the weaker A5/2 algorithm and demonstrated that only approximately 2^{16} operations, requiring no more than 10 milliseconds, were necessary to recover the key. Barkhan et al [38] later proposed a cipher-text only attack against A5/2 requiring no more than a few milliseconds to recover the key. Most recently, Hulton and Miller used FPGAs and rainbow tables to demonstrate the ability to passively recover an A5/1 key in approximately 30 seconds [111].

The alleged evolution of both encryption algorithms is also interesting. Ross Anderson, for instance, has argued that insider information revealed that politics ultimately decided the cipher used to secure voice communications in GSM systems [30]. During a meeting of the NATO signals agencies during the mid 1980's, nations argued over whether or not GSM should be protected by a strong algorithm. Countries bordering Warsaw Pact nations, especially Germany, argued that strong encryption should be used to protect communications against eavesdropping. However, the majority of other nations disagreed with this assertion and ultimately settled on a less-strong, French designed algorithm. Whether or not the details are true, the story reflects the atmosphere of fear of the widespread use of strong cryptography in the late part of the twentieth century.

Next generation cellular networks have made great leaps forward in their application of modern, publicly vetted cryptography. The descendant of GSM networks, or so-called WCDMA networks[2], use the new A5/3 algorithm. Also known as Kasumi, A5/3 is significantly stronger than its predecessors. However, research by Biham et al [42] demonstrated that the key can theoretically be recovered using $2^{54.6}$ chosen plaintexts (with a time complexity of $2^{76.1}$ Kasumi operations). Accordingly, such an attack is currently beyond practical implementation. The work by Barkhan et al [38] demonstrated that weaknesses in the protocol used by GSM networks and not Kasumi itself allow for the recovery of the key. Networks based on the CDMA2000 standard in-

---

[2] See Chapter 3 for details on the evolution of these networks.

stead now apply a derivative of AES, for which no weaknesses have yet been reported.

4.2 Vulnerabilities in the Network Core

Logical and physical isolation have been especially important to the security of the core of telecommunications networks. However, as the capabilities of and access available to the general public have expanded, so too has the ability of adversaries to gain unfettered access to critical services. In this section, we investigate some of the better known vulnerabilities in traditional and cellular telecommunications networks. These models ultimately point to a changing reality - that the security measures taken by such systems must change to reflect the reality of threats to the system.

One of the best known historical examples of a telecommunications vulnerability came as the result of the end of an era in long distance communication. Beginning in the 1940's, the AT&T network began offering many of its customers so called "direct distance dialing", or the ability to place long distance calls without the assistance of an operator. Because the technology allowing operator-free local calls was not capable of supporting long distance calling, AT&T developed a new series of protocols for carrying signaling information over the existing infrastructure. Specifically, by transmitting audio signals over the same line as voice calls, the network was able to accurately route and bill calls without human intervention. The new system spread quickly and, by the late 1950's, was deployed nearly universally across the United States. The ability to manipulate such in-band signaling from the end-points of the network was soon noticed. Nicknamed "phone phreaks", hackers with access to signal generator equipment were able to enable free long-distance calling. For example, by briefly emitting a pitch at 2600 hertz, which is the tone used by the network itself to indicated that a trunk line is not in use, an adversary could cause the network to stop billing for a call while maintaining the connection end-to-end. As the tools evolved from a cereal box toy (i.e., the Cap'n Crunch "Bosun Whistle") to the more sophisticated "Blue Box" [156], providers recognized that such an exploit could only successfully be prevented by removing in-band signaling from the network. While the vast majority of such systems were replaced digital switching systems by the mid 1980's, the vulnerabilities remained in related products. For instance, Sherr et al [165] noted in 2005 that even modern legal wire-tapping equipment could be disabled through a similar in-band audio attack. Such vulnerabilities speak directly to the evolving state of the perimeter of telecommunications networks. Specifically, the increasing availability of advanced technology to end users and vastly expanded interconnection between provider networks invalidate the many of the assumptions of an entirely controlled environment.

Increased access and interconnection with external networks creates opportunities for a much wider array of attacks than billing fraud by an individual.

The belief that modern networks retained their formerly isolated status led the designers of the current Signaling System Number 7 (SS7) network (see Chapter 3 for an in-depth overview) to design signaling protocols without any real system of authentication. Because nodes trust that all values contained in packets exchanged between network nodes, from source address to request type, an adversary with even minimal access to the SS7 infrastructure can cause significant damage to telecommunications networks nation- and even world-wide. For example, a lack of origin authentication allows messages indicating a link failure to be injected into a system, thereby forcing the network to route around (or toward) a target. Accordingly, an adversary with access to an ISDN connection or a cable can easily cause portions of the network to become unreachable or reroute all traffic toward a single victim node [117, 124]. Moreover, the cryptographic algorithms discussed in the previous section offer no protection of confidentiality in the core. Because traffic is only encrypted between a user's phone and a base station, anyone able to gain access to a cable or switch can easily eavesdrop. Attempts to mitigate such problems including MAPsec [24], which is discussed in Chapter 3, have largely been unsuccessful.

Like much of the software used on the Internet, weaknesses in the implementation of protocols in the network core have also been discovered. One of the more significant such vulnerabilities was discovered in parsers of the *Abstract Syntax Notation* (ASN.1) language. ASN.1 is used widely throughout the core of SS7 networks for tasks including call routing. However, many implementations of parsing functions fail to do sufficient input checking, thereby making a number of buffer overflow vulnerabilities exploitable. Work by researchers at Oulu University revealed that nearly every device running the SNMP protocol, which uses ASN.1 to communicate, was vulnerable to compromise. Such vulnerabilities were not simply due to the code itself, but also the compiler used to generate the parsers themselves. Many within the industry used the occasion to note that such development should leverage the knowledge of the security community [164]; however, the vast majority of systems used by telecommunications networks remain opaque to independent security researchers.

Telecommunications networks simply do not have the isolation upon which their security once relied. As the Telecommunications Act of 1996 requires [173, 161], an individual or group can connect to the SS7 infrastructure simply by paying a relatively small fee.[3] Accordingly, the security of such networks must evolve to address the changing nature of user access and behavior.

The damage possible by such attacks has already been observed in such networks, except that the source of the harm was not malicious. In 1990, AT&T updated the software in all of its 4ESS "long haul" switches. When the software on a single switch noticed that it could not correct a fault, it alerted its neighbors that it was going out of commission for four to six seconds

---

[3] In 1999, this fee was only $10,000.

to fix the problem [133]. The first communication from the problem switch to its neighbors after such a message indicated that the switch was able to process messages again. However, the new version of the software caused the neighboring switches to go into their fault mode when they received the next signal from the now functional switch. This behavior caused a cascade effect of outage in all of the switches in the network, thereby shutting down the entire long distance network in the country. Because AT&T was aware that the software caused the problem, they were able to restore service within a few hours by reinstalling an older version of the switching software. However, had an adversary instead exploited a vulnerability, similar problems in the future may not be so easily fixed.

4.3 Wireless Eavesdropping

Protecting the content of conversations sent over the air has not always been possible. Limitations in the capabilities of user devices and tight government controls on cryptography left first generation analog cellular systems such as AMPS (see Chapter 3) vulnerable to eavesdropping. Second generation cellular networks, such as GSM, were able to provide protection against direct interception by all but the most sophisticated adversaries.[4] However, poor protocol design in some modern networks can render the cryptographic protections offered by the network useless.

One of the great lessons in underestimating the capabilities of an adversary comes from the wireless portion of GSM networks. Users attempting to authenticate themselves to the system use the combination of A3 and A8 algorithms to generate the correct response and session key based on a challenge transmitted by the base station. However, the base station and therefore the network itself do not authenticate themselves to the user, allowing anyone with equipment capable of interacting with a phone the ability to pretend to be the network. Worse still, because encryption is only enabled in a negotiation after the user correctly responds to the challenge, the false base station can force the user to use the A5/0, or null, encryption algorithm. By acting as a man-in-the-middle, the presence of a false base station allows the conversation of any user to potentially be illegally monitored. While most providers initially downplayed this attack given the expense of base station equipment, an adversary could easily assemble the necessary equipment for under $10,000 [159]. While this issue has been addressed in third generation cellular networks, it should serve as a reminder that communications over the majority of current networks are in fact vulnerable.

Breaking well vetted cryptographic algorithms may not be required to gain access to conversations in reality. A number of networks can in fact

---

[4] See Section 4.1 for an examination of the weaknesses in the cryptographic algorithms used in GSM.

operate with encryption turned off entirely. For example, the A5/0 cipher in GSM networks alerts the user during connection setup that no encryption at all will be applied. Unlike the above false base station attack, the network itself may allow conversations to be exposed. Countries that legislate strict controls on cryptography, such as France, explicitly require the use of A5/0 in all GSM networks within their borders [56]. It is unknown how widespread such practices are, but rumors of the disabling encryption during periods of elevated traffic have been previously suggested. While a number of end-to-end encryption mechanisms for phones are available [202, 39], such solutions are generally limited to VoIP devices and not currently readily available to most consumers.

4.4 Jamming

When moving from a wired to a wireless transmission medium, the attack sur face of a network inherently expands. In particular, the ability of an attacker to interfere with or "jam" communications increases significantly simply by being within the transmission range of a base station. Most of the jamming technology operates by making the network's control channels, for either up-link, dowlink or both directions, unusable by phones in an area. Because the frequency of the control channel is always known to the adversary (unlike the traffic channel used in CDMA communications - see Chapter 3 for more details), all cellular networks are susceptible to attacks by an adversary with the correct radio.

Jamming technology varies significantly in its intended uses and effective range. For example, many "personal" jamming units can deny service to all users within 10 meters of the device [139, 176]. Devices used in military or counter-terrorism operations, such as the Tactical Response Jammer (TRJ) Series [32], can have effective jamming radius of up to five miles. Units with ranges somewhere between these two extremes are being used in some parts of the world to stifle calling in movie theaters, subways and other enclosed spaces.

The legality of such devices, of course, varies wildly. In the United States, for instance, the "manufacture, importation, sale or offer for sale, including advertising, of devices designed to block or jam wireless transmissions is pro-hibited" [69], as specified by the amended Telecommunications Act of 1934. Because providers are required to pay for spectrum, violation of this law is considered property theft and is punishable by fines of as much as $11,000 for the first offense and up to a year in prison for additional infractions. In spite of these restrictions, such devices are available and popular throughout the country [151]. France, alternatively, permits blocking in many of the enclosed spaces mentioned above [83]. Accordingly, jamming represents a real threat in most environments.

4.5 User Tracking and Privacy

In many circumstances, an adversary may find their target's location information more valuable than the content of their conversations. By tracking an individual's location, an adversary may be able to inflict any number of physical attacks. For instance, developing knowledge of a user's usual behaviors may allow their actions to be predicted and privacy violated. From a technological perspective, tracking a user to their bank may allow targeted attacks such as "spear phishing" to gather more effective information. Accordingly, protecting a user's identity from eavesdroppers is an important consideration for cellular networks.

Early cellular networks such as AMPS provided no protection against user tracking. To verify their identity to the network, users in the AMPS system transmitted a unique 32-bit identifier known as the *Electronic Serial Number* (ESN). However, because of the limited bandwidth of this analog system and the lack of cryptographic mechanisms on user devices, this number was broadcast in the clear. In addition to tracking users, this allowed adversaries with listening equipment to intercept ESNs and make fraudulent phone calls. This attack is said to have cost providers at least a million dollars a day in the 1990's[5] [143].

Modern digital cellular networks do not have quite the same privacy concerns. Increased device capability, in combination with increased bandwidth and the use of cryptography, make tracking individual users nearly impossible. To augment these protections further, networks such as GSM even create temporary identifiers for use over the air such that even unencrypted transmissions leak nothing about a user's identity. The growing move toward cellular phones becoming general purpose computing devices, however, presents new risks to privacy and security. Viruses and malware, as will be discussed in greater detail in Section 4.7, may purposefully leak such information to eavesdroppers. Accordingly, while the problem of user tracking has evolved, it has not evaporated from cellular networks.

4.6 Overload

Like the Internet, telecommunications are susceptible to overload conditions. Such conditions occur for a very simple reason - resources for networks simply are not allocated for worst-case scenarios in which all users want to use the service at the same time. Instead, providers typically allocate enough resources to operate within a reasonable tolerance expected load. For instance, a provider may allocate enough spectrum to handle normal rush-hour volumes plus enough extra resources to handle usage spikes as large as 20%. The

---

[5] As a note, the author's father was a victim of such an attack in New York City, and was made aware of it when the United States Secret Service contacted him in regards to phone calls made to Iraq during the first Gulf War.

cost of extra equipment and spectrum coupled with the somewhat infrequent occurrence of overload make under-utilized resources simply too expensive to maintain.

Tighter integration of these networks with the larger Internet and an expanding set of services are rapidly redefining "typical" traffic in cellular networks. Outside of the work presented in this book, a number of others have also noticed the increasing potential of this phenomenon. Soon after the attacks of September 11th, for instance, the National Communications System (NCS) issued a report on the potential of using SMS during an emergency [131]. While SMS performed admirably during the attacks in 2001, the service was largely unused by most cellular subscribers. Predicting an upswing, however, this report noted that the current infrastructure would have to be expanded by nearly 100 times to reliably support wide-scale usage of SMS during such elevated periods.

After the initial publication of our attacks, a number of other authors investigated malicious overload conditions in cellular networks. Serror et al [163], for example, noted that the effort needed address a linearly increasing set of request on the paging channels in CDMA networks grew extremely quickly. Racic et al [142] noted that phones themselves could easily be overloaded with requests targeted at draining their batteries. As we discuss in Chapter 6, the fundamental tension caused by the network's handling of data traffic will continue to reveal similar such attacks.

4.7 Malware

Viruses, worms and spyware continue to plague traditional data networks. It should therefore come as little surprise that increasing connectivity with the Internet and dramatically improved device capability have raised the specter of malware polluting cellular networks. While the impact of such malware has not yet been felt to any great extent in this environment, there is little evidence to suggest that this environment is any less susceptible.

The vast majority of viruses targeting cellular phones have not been observed "in the wild". Specifically, most such malware has been created as a proof of concept and attack a variety of services. Skulls and its variants, for example, pose as a benign Flash application and disable SMS and the *Multimedia Messaging Service* (MMS) functionality on infected Symbian Series 60 phones [66]. The Cabir worm, alternative, spreads via Bluetooth. The functionality of the worm, however, is extremely limited. For example, it requires the user to accept it being downloaded before it can infect a targeted device. Once infection occurs, the worms simply attempts to replicate itself again [62]. Commwarrior-A because the first virus to spread via MMS [64]. Mabir, a worm related to Cabir, uses the propagation methods of the previously mentioned viruses (SMS and MMS) to infect new hosts [65]. Viruses targeting other phone operating systems, such as Duts [63], have also been identified. While a number of companies currently offer antivirus software for such devices, the vast majority of users do not use such services.

Internet-based malware may also present a threat to cellular networks. Ricciato [149] surmised that the traffic generated by Internet-scale worms such as Slammer may be sufficient to accidentally deny service to users of cellular data networks. Off the record conversations with providers and equipment manufacturers have indicated that significant activity has already been observed in the other direction. Specifically, laptops equipped with GPRS modems and infected with spyware and malware cause significant and unexpected spikes in network usage and behavior. Such behavior is expected to become even more commonplace as so-called "smart" phones become the norm.

The potential for such malware to rapidly expand is greatly assisted by the number and systematic nature of the vulnerabilities in cellular-capable devices. Mulliner and Vigna [126] investigated the security of MMS agents implemented on PocketPC-based phones and discovered a number of previously unknown vulnerabilities. Through the use of fuzzing techniques, this team found a number of buffer overflow vulnerabilities in this software without gaining direct access to the source code itself. By exploiting these weaknesses, an adversary may be able to gain full control over such devices. As we discuss in Chapter 5, our own work on Symbian phones noted that few internal controls exist at all. Most critically, because the device only has a single user, all commands issued to the kernel are executed without question. Such weaknesses allowed us to develop exploits including keylogging software and will ultimately allow more powerful malware to gain complete control over a mobile phone.

5

Vulnerabilities in the Short Messaging Service (SMS)

For large portions of the population, the *Short Messaging Service* (SMS) has eclipsed voice telephony as the dominant means of communication. Noted for its discreet nature, SMS allows mobile subscribers to interact via concise, text-only messages. During its relatively short lifetime, SMS has transformed from a niche service to a system with a larger user-base than the Internet. While the benefits of this service have been tremendously positive from the perspectives of both user satisfaction and provider revenue, the inclusion of SMS in cellular networks creates significant new security issues.

In this chapter, we examine vulnerabilities created by the introduction of text messaging. Our discussion begins with an evaluation of the evolution of SMS. We then present an in-depth description of the wireless portion of the network and then discuss how competition for channels shared by both voice and text messages allows low bandwidth attacks to deny voice service to major metropolitan areas. Specifically, we apply modeling and simulation to demonstrate that an adversary with the bandwidth available to a cable modem is capable of denying service to more than 70% of calls and text messages for Manhattan. For networks in which a 1% blocking rate is unacceptable, such a degradation represents a serious operational crisis. Our investigation then turns to current countermeasures and shows why the use of "edge solutions" is not a sufficient means of preventing such attacks. We then suggest, characterize and measure the effectiveness of more appropriate mechanisms from the areas of queue management and resource provisioning.

More importantly, this chapter provides one of the first perspectives on the impact of connecting the telecommunications infrastructure and the Internet. Largely secured by its physical isolation from other systems in the past, national and international critical infrastructure are now potentially threatened by new and unpredictable attack vectors.

5.1 History and Description

The idea of a text communication mechanism as part of a cellular network was discussed widely in the early 1980's. The uses of such a service, however, varied widely. While the majority of the community imagined SMS as a mechanism to alert users of events such as voice mail and network outages, others advocated a system capable of supporting various data collection devices (e.g., telemetry). To meet the wishes all parties, the original SMS standard document (1985) [123] detailed three general functions: Short Message Mobile Terminated (from the network to the device), Short Message Mobile Originated (from a device to the network), and Short Message Cell Broadcast (from the network to all devices in an area).

Uptake of the service was slow – the first commercial text message was transmitted some seven years later in 1992 [79]. Customer use remained flat throughout until nearly the end of the decade; however, the introduction of inter-provider messaging agreements and pre-paid user plans significantly boosted the popularity of the service. By the year 2000, 5 billion messages were being sent per month. In 2005, that number increased by nearly two orders of magnitude with an estimated 1 trillion messages sent worldwide [79].

As it exists today, SMS is a text-only service that delivers message containing up to 160 characters. By default, messages are encoded in an alphabet supporting an extended Latin character set known as the GSM 7-bit default alphabet. Non-Latin character sets, including Arabic, Chinese and Russian, can be supported by an alternate 16-bit encoding. The transmission of longer messages is typically supported by splitting text into multiple messages. Complimentary services, such as MMS, can be used to support messages containing images, audio and formatting.

5.2 Delivering Messages

Before discussing vulnerabilities introduced by text messaging, we provide an overview of message delivery in a GSM network. Readers that do not possess a strong background in cellular networks are encouraged to reference Chapter 3 for additional architectural information.

5.2.1 Submitting a Message

Text messages can be sent to mobile phones via one of two general methods – from another phone or mobile device as a *mobile originated* (MO) message or through a variety of *External Short Messaging Entities* (ESMEs). ESMEs encompass devices and interfaces ranging from email and provider-run web-based messaging portals to voice mail, paging and bulk advertising systems. Whether a message is sent from another device in the network or an ESME, all messages are first processed by a *Short Messaging Service Center* (SMSC).

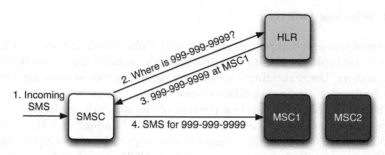

Fig. 5.1. A high-level description of text message routing. Messages 1) arrive at an SMSC from ESMEs and devices within the network. The SMSC then 2) queries the HLR to find the location of the targeted device. The HLR responds 3) with the address of the MSC serving the phone. The SMSC then 4) places the formatted message into a MAP packet and forwards it to the appropriate MSC.

These servers are responsible for the "store-and-forward" protocol that eventually delivers text messages to their intended destination. Accordingly, service providers supporting text messaging must have at least one SMSC in their network. Due to the rising popularity of this service, however, it is becoming increasingly common for service providers to support multiple SMSCs in order to increase capacity.

5.2.2 Routing a Message

When a text message arrives at an SMSC, the contents of incoming packets are examined and, if necessary, converted and copied into SMS message format. First, messages are converted into the 7-bit default alphabet, which includes all characters in the ASCII character set and a number of other accented letters [25]. The SMSC then attempts to determine the location of the targeted phone by querying the corresponding HLR with a *SendRoutingInfoForShort-Msg* request. If the targeted mobile phone is available (i.e., powered on), the HLR will respond with the address of the serving MSC. Otherwise, messages destined for unreachable are kept in the SMSC until the device becomes available. Assuming that the address of the serving MSC is returned, a MAP packet is then created and tagged with the *SMSDeliveryForward* (SMDFWD) operation specifier and forwarded. Figure 5.1 provides a high-level overview of this procedure.

When a text message arrives, the MSC begins the process of locating the targeted device. To do this, the MSC queries its associated VLR, which stores local copies of device service profiles. If the targeted device is currently in use (i.e., in a phone call), the base station nearest to the device is known and the messages is forwarded. If instead the targeted device is on but not in use, the MSC initiates the paging process described below.

5.2.3 Wireless Delivery

An area of wireless coverage is called a *cell*. Cells, which are serviced by *base stations*, are typically partitioned into multiple (usually three) smaller regions called sectors. Users standing on opposite sides of a base station are therefore likely to be operating using different resources.

The air interface, or wireless portion of the network, is divided into two general classes of logical channels – the *Control Channels* (CCHs) and *Traffic Channels* (TCHs). Traffic channels are responsible for supporting voice telephony once calls have been established. CCHs are therefore responsible for implementing all other operations necessary to run the network. Accordingly, the CCHs are partitioned into two additional classes of channels – the Common CCH and Dedicated CCHs. The Common CCH, which includes the *Broadcast Control Channel* (BCCH) is responsible for operations ranging from alerting devices of incoming calls or messages (called paging) to helping devices synchronize with the network. Accordingly, all mobile devices not currently engaged in voice or data calls periodically listen to the Common CCH. Dedicated CCHs provide information related to call setup for individual phones. As detailed below, call and SMS delivery requires the use of both classes of CCH.

When a device is not actively communicating with the network, the MSC does not keep track of the base station closest to that phone. Accordingly, upon arrival of a new call or text message, the MSC must search multiple connected base stations to locate the device. The traditional strategy to finding a phone quickly is to flood all attached base stations with paging requests. As expected, flooding requires significant resources in terms of processing power and bandwidth at the MSC. While a number of solutions reducing resource use have been proposed [27, 112], the traditional flooding mechanism is typically used in current networks because its latency and implementation complexity are low.

Each of the base stations receiving a paging message from the MSC transmits the incoming request on the *Paging Channel* (PCH). Instead of broadcasting the phone number of the targeted device, however, the network transmits a *Temporary Mobile Subscriber Identifier* (TMSI). The use of a TMSI, which is typically updated after each interaction with the network, makes tracking specific phones by wireless eavesdroppers difficult. When a device hears its TMSI broadcast on the PCH, it attempts to alert the network of its presence and availability by means of the *Random Access Channel* (RACH). The performance of this channel is discussed in greater depth in Chapter 6. Upon receiving a response, the MSC drops outstanding paging messages in other cells and the base station authenticates the phone. The base station points the phone to listen to a specific dedicated control channel via the *Access Grant Channel* (AGCH). These dedicated control channels, known as the *Standalone Dedicated Control Channels* (SDCCHs), allow the network to perform authentication via the triplet tokens described in Chapter 3, assign

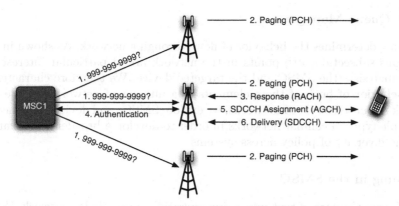

Fig. 5.2. A description of the wireless delivery process for SMS. After receiving a text message, 1) the MSC sends paging messages to multiple base stations to find the targeted phone. The base stations then 2) transmit the paging request on the PCH. When a phone hears its TMSI, 3) it responds to the base station on the RACH, which in turn 4) alerts the MSC that the phone is available and needs authentication. The base station then 5) assigns an SDCCH to the phone via the AGCH. The phone 6) then authenticates with the base station and receives the text message.

a new TMSI and deliver the contents of a text message [19]. If the network was delivering an incoming voice call instead, the delivery of an SMS message would be replaced by a pointer to a TCH upon which the call could be conducted.

We summarize these steps for simplicity in Figure 5.2.

5.3 Identifying System Bottlenecks

The closed nature of telecommunications networks makes testing specific components difficult. In spite of this, much can still be learned about these systems simply by interacting with them. In this section, we apply a technique known as gray-box testing [34, 46] to learn about the internal behavior of operational cellular networks not specified in standards documents. We characterize queuing policies, delivery rates and interfaces and demonstrate that the imbalance between resource injection and delivery rates creates the necessary precondition for a DoS attack.

Very small volumes of traffic were injected during off-peak periods in order to observe network behavior; the attack detailed in Section 5.5 was not launched against any network. Experiments damaging or disrupting such networks without the specific permission of the provider and/or government approval are illegal and should not be conducted.

5.3.1 Queue Management

Queuing determines the behavior of flows through a network. As shown in the previous subsection, two points in the network are of particular interest for such analysis – the SMSC and the targeted device. We therefore characterize the behavior of both of these elements in a number of networks. While our attack is focused on GSM networks, we explore SMSCs and devices attached to multiple types of cellular networks in order to develop a broader appreciation for the diversity of policy across systems.

Queuing in the SMSC

SMSCs are the core of text messaging operations in a cellular network. While every text message sent and received in the system passes through them, the capacity of an SMSC is limited by a number of practical considerations. Most critically, the "store-and-forward" nature of message delivery is governed by the storage capacity of the SMSC. We therefore characterize the buffering capacity and queue eviction policies to show their impact on large volumes of text messages.

The queuing and eviction policies for SMSCs were assessed by periodically sending text messages to powered-off phone. We then sent a few hundred text messages containing sequential identifiers at a rate of once per minute. The device was then powered-on and reconnected to its default network, at which time as many messages as possible were delivered. The networks of US providers AT&T[1], Verizon and Sprint were all tested using the above methodology.

Our experiments found a significant range of queuing and eviction policies. AT&T's SMSC buffered a maximum of 400 messages and delivered them in order of submission. In contrast, Verizon stored only 100 messages. More interestingly, however, Verizon discarded the first few hundred messages and delivered only the final 100. Sprint also differed from the other providers by storing only 30 messages. Like AT&T, messages sent after the user's SMSC buffer was filled experienced tail drop loss in the Sprint network.

Queuing in Phones

Mobile phones are highly constrained computing devices. Their processing ability, memory and access to power all pale in comparison to modern general purpose computing platforms. Understanding this, cellular networks allow phones to alert the network when their buffering capacity has been met. In GSM, phones send a MAP message containing the *Mobile-Station-Memory-Capacity-Exceeded-Flag* (MCEF) to the HLR [19]. When this flag is set in a

---

[1] At the time of testing, AT&T Wireless was in the initial phases of becoming Cingular Wireless. At the time of this writing, Cingular Wireless has once again become AT&T Wireless.

Table 5.1. Mobile Phone SMS Capacity

Device	Capacity (messages)
Nokia 3560	30
LG 4400	50
Treo 650	500*

* 500 messages depleted a full battery.

user's profile at the HLR, responses to *SendRoutingInfoForShortMsg* requests from the SMSC indicate that the phone is unavailable.

Determining the message storage capacity of all available phones is not practical. Instead, we selected phones exemplifying the range of capabilities available to such devices at the time of our original testing. To represent low, medium and high-end devices, we measured the capacity of a Nokia 3560 (AT&T), and LG 4400 (Verizon) and a Treo 650 with removable 1GB memory stick (Sprint), respectively. Capacity was tested by clearing all messages from the targeted device and slowly sending messages (one per minute) until the inbox was filled. As shown in Table 5.1, the capacity of both the low and medium-end phones were quickly reached. The experiments on the high-end phone resulted in a capacity of 500 messages; however, this limit is the result of the battery being drained and not the exhaustion of storage.

Implications of Queue Management

The above testing provides a number of insights into crafting targeted SMS attacks against the telecommunications infrastructure. Most importantly, the small buffers in both SMSCs and end devices suggest that large scale attacks must be distributed across multiple end devices in order to avoid overfilling SMSC and device buffers. This information also suggests that attacks targeted at individuals are also possible. Because we have shown that it is possible to cause a network to lose messages, an adversary can fill a user's SMSC queue as a means of preventing them from receiving a specific message. We investigate the implications of these observations in Section 5.5.

5.3.2 Message Injection

Key to any DoS attack is the rate at which an adversary can inject messages. In this section, we examine a sampling of the many interfaces through which targeted text messaging attacks can be launched. We use publicly available specifications to quantify conservative values for message insertion rates. Finally, we show that the imbalance between message injection and delivery time allows an adversary to use low-bandwidth attacks to impact network services.

The number of methods by which malicious text messages can be injected into a network is staggering. For instance, compromised mobile devices or those running programs with malicious side effects can create significant volumes of text messages. Given that 2.7% of cellular users download games each month [97] and a growing set of Blutoooth-based exploits [187, 62, 65], the presence of such malicious software is increasingly possible. As mentioned previously, ESMEs including service provider web interfaces, email, and instant messaging clients would open additional portals to infected PCs throughout the Internet. Even larger pipes running the *Short Messaging Peer Protocol* (SMPP) connect bulk SMS senders to the telecommunications infrastructure. With advertised rates of 30-35 messages text messages per second per client and additional services offering ten times that bandwidth [169], an adversary could hire such providers to inject significant additional messages to those sent through the free interfaces above. Given the preponderance of methods to inject text messages and individual SMSC capacities above 20,000 messages per second [29], we conservatively estimate that between several hundred and several thousand messages per second can be submitted to a network.

When the injection rate of messages exceeds the network's ability to deliver them, DoS attacks become possible. Given that SMSCs can process over 20,000 messages per second and our ability to inject several thousand messages injected per second, a superficial examination would suggest that such attacks are not possible. However, not all portions of the network are as well provisioned as the SMSCs. To illustrate this, we perform additional gray box testing and measure message injection and delivery times. For the former, we use PERL scripts that interface with the service provider web interfaces to send messages to targeted phones. An average message submission time of 0.71 seconds was recorded across all three providers. Precise measurement of delivery time were more difficult because of experimental setup (clock synchronization between the sending desktop and a phone is not a simple task). Informally, we observed an average of 7-8 seconds. These experiments demonstrate approximately an order of magnitude difference between the time required to insert a message and the time needed to delivery it.

In combination with standards information discussed in Section 5.5, the experiments conducted in this section indicate that the necessary precondition for DoS on cellular networks, an imbalance between message injection and delivery rates, is present in operational systems.

5.4 Efficient Device Targeting

The ability to successful attack on a mobile phone network requires the adversary to do more than simply attempt to send text messages to every possible phone number. Much like the creation of hit-lists for accelerated worm propagation across the Internet [168], it is possible to efficiently create a database of potential targets within a cellular phone network. The techniques below, listed from the most coarse to fine-grain methods, represent a subset of techniques for creating targeted attacks. The combination of these and other methods can be used to create extremely accurate hit-lists.

The most obvious first step would be simply to attempt to capture phone numbers overheard on the air interface. Because of the use of TMSIs over the air interface, this approach is not possible[2]. We therefore look to the web as our source of data.

5.4.1 NPA/NXX

The United States, Canada, and 18 other nations throughout the Caribbean adhere to the *North American Numbering Plan* (NANP) for telephone number formatting. NANP phone numbers consist of ten digits, which are traditionally represented as "NPA-NXX-XXXX[3]". These digit groupings represent the area code or *Numbering Plan Area*, exchange code[4], and terminal number, respectively. Traditionally, all of the terminal numbers for a given NPA/NXX prefix are administered by a single service provider.

A quick search of the Internet yields a number of websites with access to the NPA/NXX database. Responses to queries include the name of the service provider administering that NPA/NXX domain, the city where that domain is located and the subdivision of NPA/NXX domains among a number of providers. For example, in the greater State College, PA region, 814-876-XXXX is owned by AT&T Wireless; 814-404-XXXX is managed by Verizon Wireless; 814-769-XXXX is supervised by Sprint PCS.

This information is useful to an attacker as it reduces the size of the domain to strictly numbers administered by wireless providers within a given region; however, this data does not give specific information in regards to which of the terminals within the NPA/NXX have been activated. Furthermore, as of November 23, 2004, this method does not account for numbers within a specific NPA/NXX domain that have been transferred to another carrier under new number portability laws. Nonetheless, this approach is extremely powerful when used in conjunction with other methods, as it reduces the amount of address space needed to be probed.

5.4.2 Web Scraping

As observed in the Internet, a large number of messages sent to so-called "dark address space" is a strong indicator that an attack is in progress. A more refined use of domain data, however, is readily available.

---

[2] It may be possible to match TMSIs to a specific user if the adversary can overhear an initial assignment. During this exchange, the IMSI is transmitted without encryption.

[3] Numbers in the last two subsets can take the form of N(2-9) or X(0-9)

[4] The "NXX" portion of a phone number is sometimes referred to as the "NPX" or *Numbering Plan Exchange*.

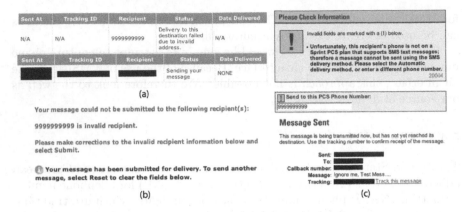

Fig. 5.3. The negative (top) and positive (bottom) response messages created by message submission to a) Verizon, b) Cingular and c) Sprint PCS. Black rectangles have been added to preserve sensitive data.

Web Scraping is a technique commonly used by spammers to collect information on potential targets. Through the use of search engines and scripting tools, these individuals are able to gather email addresses posted on web pages in an efficient, automated fashion. These same search tools can easily be harnessed to collect mobile phone numbers listed across the web. For example, the query `Cell 999-999-0000..9999` at Google yields a large number of hits for the entire range of the NPA/NXX "999-999-XXXX". Through our own proof-of concept scripts, we were able to collect 865 unique numbers from the greater State College, PA region, 7,308 from New York City and 6,184 from Washington D.C. with minimal time and effort.

The difficulty with this method, much like the first, is that it does not give a definitive listing of numbers that are active and those that are not. As personal web pages are frequently neglected, the available information is not necessarily up to date. Accordingly, some portion of these numbers could have long since been returned to the pool of dark addresses. Furthermore, due to number porting, there is no guarantee that these numbers are still assigned to the service provider originally administering that domain. Regardless, this approach significantly narrows down the search space of potential targets.

5.4.3 Testing Phone "Liveness"

All of the major providers of wireless service in the United States offer a website interface through which anyone can, at no charge to the sender, submit SMS messages. If a message created through this interface is addressed to a subscriber of this particular provider, the message is sent to the targeted mobile device and a positive acknowledgment is delivered to the sender. A message is rejected from the system and the user, depending on the provider, is returned an error message if the targeted device is a subscriber of a different provider or is addressed to a user that has opted to turn off text messaging services. An example of the both the positive and negative acknowledgments is available in Figure 5.3. Of the service providers tested (AT&T Wireless, Cingular, Nextel, Sprint PCS, T-Mobile and Verizon Wireless[5]), only AT&T did not respond with a positive or negative acknowledgment; however, it should be noted that subscribers of AT&T Wireless are slowly being transitioned over to Cingular due to its recent acquisition.

The positive and negative acknowledgments can be used to create an extremely accurate hit-list for a given NPA/NXX domain. Every positive response generated by the system identifies a potential future target. Negative responses can be interpreted in multiple ways. For example, if the number corresponding to a negative response was found through web scraping, it may instead be tried again at another provider's website. If further searching demonstrates a number as being unassigned, it can be removed from the list of potential future targets.

While an automated, high speed version of this method of hit-list creation may be noticed for repeated access to dark address space, an infrequent querying of these interfaces over a long period of time (i.e., a "low and slow" attack) would be virtually undetectable.

A parallel result could instead be accomplished by means of an automated dialing system; however, the simplicity of code writing and the ability to match a phone to a specific provider makes a web-interface the optimal candidate for building hit-lists in this fashion.

5.4.4 Additional Collection Methods

A number of specific techniques can also be applied to hit-list development. For example, a worm could be designed to collect stored phone numbers from victim devices by address book scraping. In order to increase the likelihood that a list contained only valid numbers, the worm could instead be programmed to take only the numbers from the "Recently Called" list. The effectiveness of his method would be limited to mobile devices running specific operating systems. The interaction between many mobile devices and desktop computers could also be exploited. An Internet worm designed to scrape the contents of a synchronized address book and then post that data to a public location such as a chat room would yield similar data. Lastly, Bluetooth enabled devices have become notorious for leaking information. Hidden in a busy area such as a bus, subway or train terminal, a device designed to collect this sort of information [187, 180] through continuous polling of Bluetooth-enabled mobile phones in the vicinity would quickly be able to create a large and temporally

---

[5] Since the original experiments, the above providers have changed. AT&T Wireless was absorbed by Cingular, which recently changed its name back to AT&T. Sprint and Nextel have also merged into a single entity.

accurate hit-list. If this system was left to run for a number of days, a correlation could be drawn between a phone number and a location given a time and day of the week.

5.5 Modeling Denial of Service

Given the existing bottlenecks and the ability to create hit-lists, we now discuss attacks against cellular networks. An adversary can mount an attack by simultaneously sending messages through the numerous available portals into the SMS network. The resulting aggregate load saturates the control channels thereby blocking legitimate voice and SMS communication. Depending on the size of the attack, the use of these services can be denied for targets ranging in size from major metropolitan areas to entire continents.

5.5.1 Attacking Individuals

In 2002, anonymous individuals inundated spammer Alan Ralsky with thousands of mail-order catalogs on a daily basis. Through the use of simple scripting tools [48], these individuals subscribed Ralsky to postal mailing lists at a much faster rate than he could possibly be removed. In so doing, Ralsky's ability to receive normal postal mail at his primary residence was all but destroyed.

Similar attacks on text messages are also possible. Given the SMSC queue management policies discovered in Section 5.3.1, an adversary can prevent a victim from receiving useful messages. For example, a jealous ex-lover may wish to keep a message from being delivered; a stock trader may want to delay updates received by competitors; an attacker may want to keep a systems administrator from receiving a notification.

This attack is accomplished by flooding the user with messages. This results in one of three outcomes: a buffer somewhere overfills and the message is lost, the message is delayed longer than its shelf-life[6], or the user does not notice the message due to the deluge of meaningless messages.

In many cases, an attack allowing intentional message loss is ideal for the adversary. Mobile phones, like other embedded devices, have significant memory constraints, thereby limiting the number of messages a phone can hold. Once the phone can no longer receive messages, the service provider's network begins to buffers all subsequent messages. For reasons of practicality, providers impose limitations on the number of messages the network can store per user. Thus, if the adversary can exceed this value, messages become lost.

Message loss can occur throughout the network. As observed with the Nokia 3560, when the buffer became full, any previously read messages were automatically deleted. While this occurrence was isolated to the firmware of

---

[6] An SMS weather notification is useless if you are already stuck in the rain.

a specific phone, the potential to remotely maliciously destroy a user's data exists.

The onslaught of large numbers of packets helps accomplish the remaining two attack outcomes. During our gray-box testing in Section 5.3.1, the delivery of all 400 packets stored in the SMSC took almost 90 minutes even with the constant monitoring and clearing of phone buffers. Temporally critical messages were potentially delayed beyond their period of usefulness. Additionally, the use of the "Clear Inbox" function significantly increases the possibility of a user accidentally deleting a legitimate text message that arrived among the attack messages.

While deleting an immense number of text messages is taxing on the user, the receipt of large amounts of data consumes significant battery power. This leads to yet another targeted DoS attack, a battery depletion attack. After the publication of our original work, Racic et al. [142] discussed a similar battery depletion attack using the data network.

5.5.2 Metropolitan Area Service

As discussed in Section 5.2, the wireless portion of SMS delivery begins when the targeted device hears its *Temporary Mobile Subscriber ID* (TMSI) over the *Paging Channel* (PCH). The phone acknowledges the request via the *Random Access Channel* (RACH) and then proceeds with authentication and content delivery over a *Standalone Dedicated Control Channel* (SDCCH).

Voice call establishment is very similar to SMS delivery, except a *Traffic Channel* (TCH) is allocated for voice traffic at the completion of control signaling. The advantage of this approach is that SMS and voice traffic do not compete for TCHs, which are held for significantly longer periods of time. Therefore, TCH use can be optimized such that the maximum number of concurrent calls is provided. Because both voice and SMS traffic use the same channels for session establishment, contention for these limited resources still occurs. Given enough SMS messages, the channels needed for session establishment will become saturated, thereby preventing voice traffic to a given area. Such a scenario is not merely theoretical; instances of this contention have been well documented [78, 72, 50, 120, 136, 98].

In order to determine the required number of messages to induce saturation, the details of the air interface must be examined. While the following analysis of this vulnerability focuses on GSM networks, other systems (e.g. CDMA [172]) appear to be vulnerable to similar attacks.

The GSM air interface is a timesharing system. This technique is commonly employed in a variety of systems to provide an equal distribution of resources between multiple parties. Each channel is divided into eight timeslots and, when viewed as a whole, form a frame. During a given timeslot on a *Transmission Channel* (TRX), the assigned user receives full control of the channel. From the telephony perspective, a user assigned to a given TCH is able to transmit voice data once per frame. In order to provide the illusion

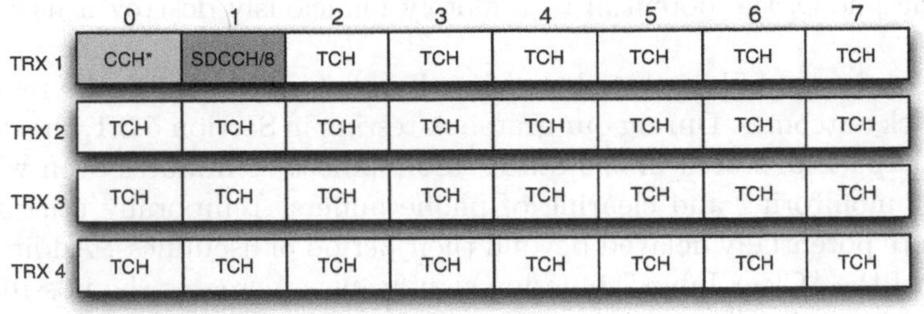

	0	1	2	3	4	5	6	7
TRX 1	CCH*	SDCCH/8	TCH	TCH	TCH	TCH	TCH	TCH
TRX 2	TCH	TCH	TCH	TCH	TCH	TCH	TCH	TCH
TRX 3	TCH	TCH	TCH	TCH	TCH	TCH	TCH	TCH
TRX 4	TCH	TCH	TCH	TCH	TCH	TCH	TCH	TCH

Fig. 5.4. An example air interface with four carriers (each showing a single frame). The first time slot of the first carrier is the Common CCH. The second time slot of the first channel is reserved for SDCCH connections. Over the course of a multiframe, capacity for eight users is allotted. The remaining time slots across all carriers are designated for voice data. This setup is common in many urban areas.

of continuous voice sampling, the frame length is limited to 4.615 ms. An illustration of this system is shown in Figure 5.4.

Because the bandwidth within a given frame is limited, data (especially relating to the CCH) must often span a number of frames, as depicted in Figure 5.5. This aggregation is known as a multiframe and is typically comprised of 51 frames[7]. For example, over the course of a single multiframe, the base station is able to dedicate up to 34 of the 51 Common CCH slots to paging operations.

Each channel has distinct characteristics. While the PCH is used to signal each incoming call and text message, its commitment to each session is limited to the transmission of a TMSI. TCHs, on the other hand, remain occupied for the duration of a call, which on average is a number of minutes [131]. The SDDCH, which has approximately the same bandwidth as the PCH across a multiframe, is occupied for a number of seconds per session establishment. Accordingly, in many scenarios, this channel can become a bottleneck.

In order to determine the characteristics of the wireless bottleneck, it is necessary to understand the available bandwidth. As shown in Figure 5.5, each SDCCH spans four logically consecutive timeslots in a multiframe. With 184 bits per control channel unit and a multiframe cycle time of 235.36 ms, the effective bandwidth is 782 bps [16]. Given that authentication, TMSI renewal, the enabling of encryption, and the 160 byte text message must be transferred, a single SDCCH is commonly held by an individual session for between four and five seconds [131]. The gray-box testing in Section 5.3 reinforces the plausibility of this value by observing no messages delivered in under six seconds.

This service time translates into the ability to handle up to 900 SMS sessions per hour on each SDCCH. In real systems, the total number of SDCCHs

---

[7] Multiframes can actually contain 26, 51 or 52 frames. A justification for each case is available in the standards [16].

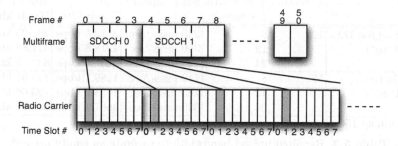

Fig. 5.5. Timeslot 1 from each frame in a multiframe creates the logical SDCCH channel. In a single multiframe, up to eight users can receive SDCCH access.

available in a sector is typically equal to twice the number of carriers[8], or one per three to four voice channels. For example, in an urban location such as the one demonstrated in Figure 5.4 where a total of four carriers are used, a total of eight SDCCHs are allocated. A less populated suburban or rural sector may only have two carriers per area and therefore have four allocated SDCCHs. Densely populated metropolitan sectors may have as many as six carriers and therefore support up to 12 SDCCHs per area.

We now calculate the maximum capacity of the system for an area. As indicated in a study conducted by the *National Communications System* (NCS) [131], the city of Washington D.C. has 40 cellular towers and a total of 120 sectors. This number reflects sectors of approximately 0.5 to 0.75 mi² through the 68.2 mi² city. Assuming that each of the sectors has eight SDCCHs, the total number of messages per second needed to saturate the SDCCH capacity C is:

$$C \simeq (120 \text{ sectors}) \left(\frac{8 \text{ SDCCH}}{1 \text{ sector}} \right) \left(\frac{900 \text{ msgs/hr}}{1 \text{ SDCCH}} \right)$$

$$\simeq 864,000 \text{ msgs/hr}$$

$$\simeq 240 \text{ msgs/sec}$$

Manhattan is smaller in area at 31.1 mi². Assuming the same sector distribution as Washington D.C., there are 55 sectors. Due to the greater population density, we assume 12 SDCCHs are used per sector.

---

[8] Actual allocation of SDCCH channels may vary across implementations; however, these are the generally accepted values throughout the community.

Area	# Sectors	# SDCCHs per sector	SMS Capacity	Upload Bandwidth*	Multi-Recipient Bandwidth*
Washington D.C. (68.2 mi^2)	120	8	240 msgs/sec	2812.5 kbps	281.25 kbps
		12	360 msgs/sec	4218.8 kbps	421.88 kbps
		24	720 msgs/sec	8437.5 kbps	843.75 kbps
Manhattan (31.1 mi^2)	55	8	110 msgs/sec	1289.1 kbps	128.91 kbps
		12	165 msgs/sec	1933.6 kbps	193.66 kbps
		24	330 msgs/sec	3867.2 kbps	386.72 kbps

* assuming 1500 bytes per message

Table 5.2. Required upload bandwidth to saturate an empty network

$$C \simeq (55 \text{ sectors}) \left(\frac{12 \text{ SDCCH}}{1 \text{ sector}} \right) \left(\frac{900 \text{ msg/hr}}{1 \text{ SDCCH}} \right)$$

$$\simeq 594,000 \text{ msg/hr}$$

$$\simeq 165 \text{ msg/sec}$$

Given that SMSCs in use by service providers in 2002 were capable of processing 20,000 messages per second [29], such volumes are achievable even in the *hypothetical* case of a sector having twice this number of SDCCHs.

Using a source transmission size of 1500 bytes to submit an SMS from the Internet, Table 5.2 shows the bandwidth required at the source to saturate the control channels, thereby incapacitating legitimate voice and text messaging services for Washington D.C. and Manhattan. The adversary's bandwidth requirements can be reduced by an order of magnitude when attacking providers including Verizon and Cingular Wireless due to the ability to have a single message repeated to up to ten recipients.

As mentioned in Section 5.3.1, sending this magnitude of messages to a small number of recipients would degrade the effectiveness of such an attack. Targeted phones would quickly see their buffers reach capacity. Undeliverable messages would then be buffered in the network until the space allotted per user was also exhausted. These accounts would likely be flagged and potentially temporarily shut down for receiving a high number of messages in a short period of time, thereby fully extinguishing the attack. Clever usage of well constructed hit-lists keeps the number of messages seen by individual phones far below realistic thresholds for rate limitation on individual targets.

Using the conservative population and demographic numbers cited from the NCS technical bulletin [131][9] and assuming 50% of the wireless subscribers in Washington are serviced by the same network, an even distribution of messages would require the delivery of approximately 5.04 messages to each phone per hour (1 message every 11.92 minutes) to saturate Washington D.C. If the

---

[9] 572,059 people with 60% wireless penetration and 8 SDCCHs (and that devices are powered on).

percentage of subscribers receiving service from a provider is closer to 25%, the number is only 10.07 messages per hour (1 message every 5.96 minutes). In a more densely populated city such as Manhattan, with a population estimated at 1,318,000 with 60% wireless penetration and 12 SDCCHs, only 1.502 messages would have to be received per user per hour if half of the wireless clientele use the same provider. That number increases slightly to 3.01 if the number is closer to 25%.

Depending on the intended duration of an attack, the creation of very large hit-lists may not be necessary. An adversary may only require a five minute service outage to accomplish their mission. Assuming that the attacker created a hit-list with only 2500 phone numbers, with each target having a buffer of 50 messages and launched their attack in a city with 8 SDCCHs (e.g., Washington D.C.), uniform random use of the hit-list would deliver a single message to each phone every 10.4 seconds, allowing the attack to last 8.68 minutes before buffer exhaustion. Similar to the most dangerous worms in the Internet, this attack could be completed before anyone capable of thwarting it could respond.

When compared to the requisite bandwidth to launch these attacks listed in Table 5.2, many of these scenarios can be executed from a single high-end cable modem. A more distributed, less bandwidth intense attack might instead be launched from a *small* zombie network or from a number of compromised mobile phone or from a number of compromised mobile phones.

While the disruption of voice and SMS service is achievable through frequency jamming attacks, physical proximity to a target is required. The danger of the attacks discussed in this chapter is their ability to be launched from any point on the globe without the perpetrator ever having been present in the targeted area.

5.5.3 Regional Service

Both popularity and the potential for high revenue have forced service providers to investigate methods of increasing SMS capacity in their networks. Already, a number of major industrial players [51, 87] offer solutions designed to offload SMS traffic from the traditional SS7 phone system onto less expensive, higher bandwidth IP-based networks. New SMSCs, each capable of processing some 20,000 SMS messages per second, would help to quickly disseminate the constantly increasing demand.

Advanced services including *General Packet Radio Service* (GPRS) and *Enhanced Data rates for GSM Evolution* (EDGE) promise high speed data connections to the Internet for mobile devices. While offering to alleviate multimedia traffic at the SMSC and potentially send some SMS messages, these data services are widely viewed as complimentary to SMS and will thus not replace SMS's functionality in the foreseeable future [45][10]. In terms of

---

[10] SMS over GPRS is already in service; however, it is not the default method of SMS delivery on GPRS-capable phones and must be activated by the user. Fur-

SMS delivery, all aspects of the network are increasing available bandwidth except the SDCCH bottleneck. A discussion of vulnerabilities in these higher bandwidth services is given in Chapter 6.

We examine a conservative attack on the cellular infrastructure in the United States. From the United States Census in 2000, approximately 92,505 mi^2[188] are considered urban. This 2.62% of the land is home to approximately 80% of the nation's population. We first model the attack by assuming that all urban areas in the country have high-capacity sectors (8 SDCCHs per sector). This assumption leads to the results shown below:

$$C \simeq \left(\frac{8 \text{ SDCCH}}{1 \text{ sector}}\right)\left(\frac{900 \text{ msg/hr}}{1 \text{ SDCCH}}\right)\left(\frac{1.7595 \text{ sectors}}{1 \text{ mi}^2}\right)$$
$$(92,505 \text{ mi}^2)$$
$$\simeq 1,171,890,342 \text{ msg/hr}$$
$$\simeq 325,525 \text{ msg/sec}$$

This attack would require approximately 3.8 Gbps and a nation-wide hit-list to be successful. If the adversary is able to submit a single message to up to ten different recipients, the requisite bandwidth for the attacker drops to approximately 370 Mbps. Considering that previous *Distributed Denial of Service* (DDoS) attacks have crippled websites such as Yahoo! with gigabits per second bandwidth, an attack on the entire cellular infrastructure is within the capability of sophisticated adversaries.

5.6 Network Characterization

The calculations in the previous section offer only coarse-grained approximations of targeted text messaging attacks. For instance, the subtle interplay of realistic traffic patterns with a host of network components are not captured. Without unrestricted access to an operational cellular network, characterizing the behavior of specific components is difficult. In order to accurately characterize the impact of such an attack on the air interface, we have developed a detailed GSM simulator. We base our system behavior and parameter settings on publicly available standards documents [17, 16].

A cellular deployment similar to that found in Manhattan [131] is used as our baseline scenario. Each of the 55 sectors in the city has 12 SDCCHs[11]. We assume both call requests and text messages arrive with a Poisson distribution

---

thermore, SMS over GPRS still defaults to the standard SMS delivery mechanism when GPRS is unavailable

[11] In reality, only the highest capacity sectors would be so over-provisioned [131], making this a conservative estimate for every sector in a city.

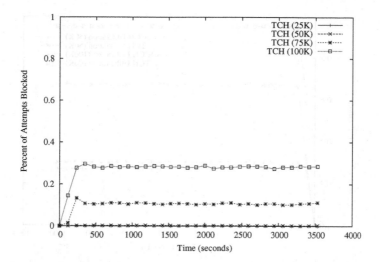

Fig. 5.6. Blocking characteristics of a network under a variety of traffic intensities.
and that TCH and SDCCH holding times are exponentially distributed around
the appropriate means (see Table 5.3) unless explicitly stated otherwise. Such
values are well within standard operating conditions [118, 125, 119].

Figure 5.6 illustrates the blocking rates for traffic channels under four
different voice traffic loads. Most relevant to the current discussion is the
nonexistence of call blocking. The absence of such blocking reinforces the
robustness of the design of GSM as a voice communication system. Specifically,
the only points of congestion in the system are the traffic channels themselves.
Figure 5.7 further supports the blocking data by illustrating very low SDCCH
utilization rates for offered loads of both 50 and 100K *calls/hour*.

Elevated loads may represent significant public gatherings (e.g., concerts,
celebrations), holiday spikes or large-scale emergencies. Blocking on other
channels begins to become observable only under such extreme circumstances.
Figure 5.8 highlights an emergency situation in which the call and SMS rate

Table 5.3. System and Attack Parameters

μ_{TCH}^{-1}	120 sec [135]
$\mu_{SDCCH,call}^{-1}$	1.5 sec [135]
$\mu_{SDCCH,SMS}^{-1}$	4 sec [131]
λ_{call}	50,000 calls/city/hr .2525 calls/sector/sec
$\lambda_{SMS,attack}$	495 msgs/city/sec 9 msgs/sector/sec
$\lambda_{SMS,regular}$	138.6K/city/hr 0.7 msgs/sector/sec

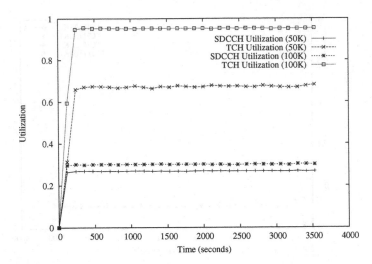

Fig. 5.7. Channel utilization characteristics of a network under a variety of traffic intensities.

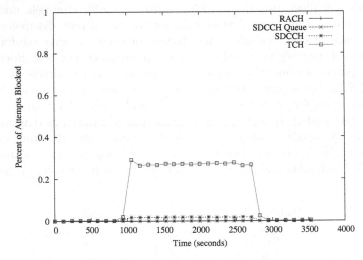

Fig. 5.8. Blocking characteristics of a network under emergency conditions (100K calls/hr, 276K msgs/hour).

spikes from 50K *calls/hour* to 100K *calls/hour* and 138K *msgs/hour* to 276K *msgs/hour*, respectively. Figure 5.9, which shows the channel utilization data for the "emergency" scenario, reinforces that it is only under extreme duress that other channels in the system begin to saturate.

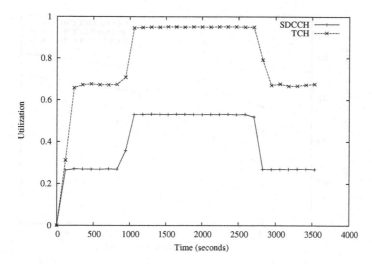

Fig. 5.9. Channel utilization characteristics of a network under emergency conditions (100K calls/hr, 276K msgs/hour).

5.7 Attack Characterization

In order to judge the efficacy of any countermeasure against targeted SMS attacks, it is necessary to fully characterize such an event. We seek to understand the observed conditions and the subtle interplay of network components given a wide range of inputs. We use the simulator described in the previous subsection and the parameters in Table 5.3 to understand such attacks.

To isolate the impact of blocking caused by SDCCH congestion, we do not include SDCCH queues; we examine the impact of such queues in Section 5.9. If a call request or text message arrives when all SDCCHs are occupied, the request is blocked.

A sector is observed for a total of 60 minutes, in which the middle 30 minutes are exposed to a targeted SMS attack. The SMS attack intensity is varied between 4 and 13 times the normal SMS load, i.e., $\lambda_{SMS} = 165 \ msgs/sec$ (3 messages/second/sector) to $\lambda_{SMS} = 495 \ msgs/sec$ (9 messages/second/sector)[12]. All results are the average of 1000 runs, each using randomly generated traffic patterns consistent with the above parameters.

Because delay variability is likely throughout the network, and because SDCCH holding times will not be deterministic due to varying processing times and errors on the wireless links, the perfect attack presented in our previous work would be difficult to achieve in real networks. Accordingly, we investigate a number of flow arrival characteristics while considering exponentially

---

[12] Because DoS attacks on the Internet frequently exhibit more than an entire year's volume of traffic [150], such an increase is relatively insignificant.

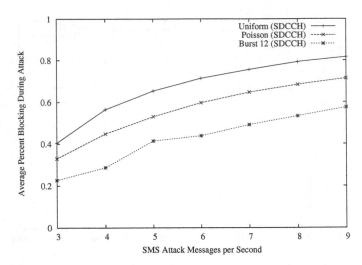

Fig. 5.10. The blocking probability for traffic exhibiting uniform, Poisson and bursty arrival patterns over varying attack strengths.

distributed SDCCH holding times. Figure 5.10 illustrates the effectiveness of attacks when messages arrive with a Poisson, bursty (12 messages delivered back-to-back), or uniform distribution. Notice that, due to the addition of variability, bursty attacks are the least successful of the three. This is because it is unlikely that 12 text messages arriving back-to-back will all find unoccupied SDCCHs. Thus, blocking occurs on the attack messages, and legitimate traffic that arrives between bursts has a higher probability of finding an available SDCCH. The most effective attack is when messages arrive uniformly spaced; however, due to variable network delay, such an attack would also be difficult to realize.

Our remaining experiments therefore assume a Poisson distribution for the arrival of text messages. We use an attack intensity of 495 $msgs/sec$, which is equal to 9 messages/second/sector and yields a blocking probability of 71%. For this case we show the SDCCH and TCH utilization in Figure 5.11. This figure shows the effectiveness of the attack: during the attack, the SDCCH utilization is near 1.0, and the TCH utilization drops from close to 70% down to approximately 20%. This shows that although TCHs are available for voice calls, they cannot be allocated due to SDCCH congestion. Our experiments suggest that, at this rate, no other bottlenecks in the system exist, including other control channels or the SS7 signaling links.

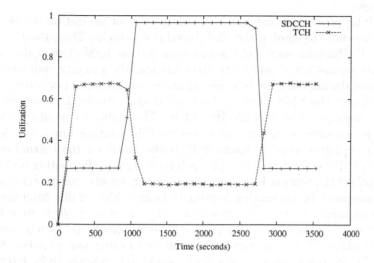

Fig. 5.11. The utilization of SDCCHs and TCHs for an attack exhibiting a Poisson interarrival at a rate of 495 messages/second.

5.8 Current Solutions

Voice communications have traditionally received priority in telecommunications systems. Because voice has been the dominant means by which people interact via these networks, providers allow for the degradation of other services in order to achieve high availability for the voice services. There are, however, an increasing set of scenarios in which the priority of services begins to change.

On September 11th, 2001, service providers experienced significant surges in usage. Verizon Wireless reported the number of calls made increased by more than 100% above average levels. Cingular Wireless experienced an increase of over 1000% for calls bound for the greater Washington D.C area [131]. In spite of the increased call volume, SMS messages were still received in even the most inundated areas because the control channels used for their delivery remained uncongested. In both emergency and day-to-day situations, the utility of text messaging has increased to the same level as voice communications for significant portions of the population [4].

A simple analysis shows that repurposing all resources used in voice telephony for SMS delivery would greatly increase overall network throughput. Specifically, more users would be able to communicate concurrently under such a scheme. However, regulations constraining the availability of voice services during times of emergency prevent such an approach from being implemented. Given requirements for reliable voice and an ever-increasing demand for and reliance upon SMS, mitigation strategies must not only maintain the availability of voice services, but also maximize the throughput of legitimate text messages.

Cellular providers have introduced a number of mitigation solutions into phone networks to combat the SMS-based DoS attacks. These solutions focus on *rate limiting* the source of the messages and are ineffective against all but the least sophisticated adversary. To illustrate, the primary countermeasure discovered during our gray-box testing in Section 5.3 was a per-source volume restriction at the SMS gateway. Such restrictions would, for example, allow only 50 messages from a single IP address. The ability to spoof IP addresses and the existence of bot networks render this solution impotent. Another popular deployed solution filters SMS traffic based on the textual content. Similar to SPAM filtering, this approach is effective in eliminating undesirable traffic only if the content is predictable. However, an adversary can bypass this countermeasure by generating legitimate looking SMS traffic from randomly generated simple texts, e.g., *"Remember to pick up your shirts from the dry cleaner on your way home. -Alice"*. As a proof of concept, we used text samples from provider "Terms of Service" documents during our gray-box testing. None of these randomly chosen strings caused any message to be filtered.

Note that these and the overwhelming majority of other solutions deployed in response to the SMS vulnerability can be classified as *edge solutions*[13]. Ineffective by construction because of their lack of context, such solutions try to regulate the traffic flowing from the Internet into the provider network at its edge. Limiting the total volume of traffic coming across all interfaces results simply in reduced income under normal operating conditions. For example, a total of 1,000 email-generated text messages per second distributed across a nation cause no ill effects to the network and generates significant revenue. As is shown in Section 5.7, such a volume of traffic is more than sufficient to deny service to Manhattan. If a provider were to limit the number of messages to a much smaller number (e.g., 250 messages per second from the Internet), the adversary could simply tighten their targeted attack area so that this volume of messages continued to elicit the same effect. Moreover, an adversary compromising a large number of mobile phones could bypass such edge solutions completely as the source of the attack would be located within the network.

Rate limitation is largely unattractive even within the core network. The distributed nature of SMSCs, through which all text messages flow, makes it difficult to coordinate real-time filtering in response to targeted attacks. In addition, because provider networks cover huge geographic areas and consist of hundreds of thousands of network elements, any compromised element can be a conduit for malicious traffic. If left unregulated, the connections between provider networks can also be exploited to inject SMS traffic.

It is therefore prudent to assume that an adversary is able to successfully submit a large number of text messages into a cellular network. The

---

[13] This class of solutions is designed to protect the "edge" of the network

Table 5.4. Commonly Used Variables

λ_{call}	Arrival rate of voice calls
λ_{SMS}	Arrival rate of text messages
$\mu_{SDCCH,call}$	Service rate of voice calls at SDCCH
$\mu_{TCH,call}$	Service rate of voice calls at TCH
$\mu_{SDCCH,SMS}$	Service rate of text messages at SDCCH
ρ_{call}	Call traffic intensity
ρ_{SMS}	SMS traffic intensity

defenses discussed in the following sections are dedicated to protecting the resource that is being exploited in the SMS attack – the bandwidth constrained
SDCCHs. Note that the Internet faces a similar conundrum: once dominant
perimeter defenses are failing in the face of dissolving network borders, e.g., as
caused by wireless connectivity and larger and more geographically distributed
networks [114]. While we certainly recognize that edge solutions provide some
barrier to attack by filtering out obvious SPAM, the approaches below provide
a "defense in depth" approach to protect telecommunications networks.

5.9 Queue Management

While the solutions currently in place are not sufficient to prevent targeted
text messaging attacks, the application of other well-known techniques has
great potential. A variety of queue management mechanisms, for example,
have been extensively investigated and tested in IP networks. As a first step
towards mitigating targeted text messaging attacks, we apply variants of two
of the more prominent techniques from this area – Weighted Fair Queuing
and Weighted Random Early Discard. Because the environment in which these
solutions are applied is significantly different from an IP network, the behavior
of these solutions is not entirely as expected.

To assist those readers not familiar with queuing theory, Table 5.4 provides
definitions for the variables used throughout the remainder of this chapter.

5.9.1 Weighted Fair Queuing

Analysis

Because we cannot rely on rate limitation at the source of messages, we now
explore network-based solutions. Fair Queuing [129] is a scheduling algorithm
that separates flows into individual queues and then apportions bandwidth
equally between them. Designed to emulate bit-wise interleaving, Fair Queuing
services queues in a round-robin fashion. Packets are transmitted when their
calculated interleaved finishing time is the shortest. Building priority into such
a system is a simple task of assigning weights to flows. Known as *Weighted*

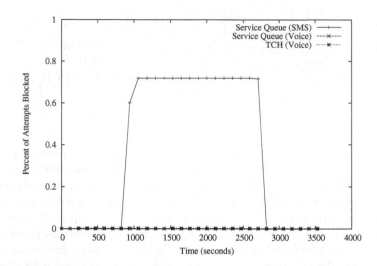

Fig. 5.12. The simulated blocking probability for a sector implementing WFQ. Notice that voice calls are unaffected by the attack, whereas the majority of text messages are dropped.

Fair Queuing (WFQ) [57], this technique can be used to give incoming voice calls priority over SMS.

We provide a simplified analysis to characterize the performance of WFQ in this scenario. We apply WFQ to the service queues of the SDDCH. We create two waiting queues, one for voice requests and one for SMS requests, respectively. The size of the call queue is 6 and the size of the SMS queue is 12 in order to buffer small bursts but to limit call processing latency. To determine the relative blocking probability and utilization of the voice and SMS flows, we begin by assuming the conditions set forth in Tables 5.4 and 5.3.

WFQ can be approximated as a *General Processor Sharing* system (GPS) [162]. The average service rate of such systems is the weighted average of the service rates of all classes of service requests. In our case we have two types of requests: voice calls with $\lambda_{call} = 0.2525$ *calls/sector/sec* and an average service time on the SDCCH of $\mu_{call}^{-1} = 1.5$ seconds, and SMS requests with $\lambda_{SMS} = 9.7$ *msgs/sector/sec* (attack traffic + regular traffic) and $\mu_{SMS}^{-1} = 4$ seconds. Therefore, for our system, $\mu^{-1} = 3.94$ seconds.

Although our system has multiple servers (SDCCHs), and is thus an M/M/n system, because it is operating at high loads during an attack, it may be approximated by an M/M/1 system with its $\mu = n\mu'$, where μ' is the service rate calculated above. Using these values, and accounting for the weighting of 2:1 for servicing call requests, the call traffic intensity $\lambda_{call}/\mu_{call} = \rho_{call} = 0.04$, and the expected call queue occupancy is about 1%. Because the ρ_{SMS} is much greater than 1, its SMS queue occupancy is

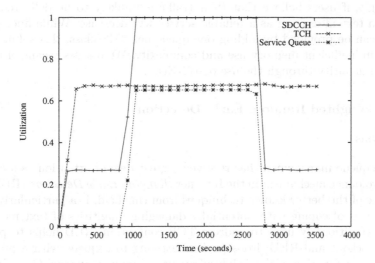

Fig. 5.13. Utilization for a sector implementing WFQ. Note that TCH utilization is constant throughout the attack.

approximately 100%. When combined, the total queue occupancy is approximately 67%.

Simulation

Buffering alone is not sufficient to protect against congestion [129, 99]; rather, mechanisms designed to mediate tail drop blocking are necessary. We apply WFQ with a weight of 2 for calls and 1 for SMS messages to ensure voice calls receive a suitable amount of SDCCH bandwidth.

Figure 5.12 illustrates the resulting blocking for a sector implementing WFQ. The preferential treatment of voice traffic eliminates the blocking previously seen in an unprotected system. Incoming text messages, however, continue to experience roughly the same blocking (72%) observed by all traffic in the base attack scenario. As is shown in Figure 5.13, the queue itself does nothing to prevent congestion. Total queue utilization is 65%. As two-thirds of the queue space is available to text messaging, this represents a near total average occupancy of the SMS queue and a virtually unused voice traffic queue. Such an observation conforms to our analytical results. This figure also demonstrates the ability to protect voice services, as TCH utilization is not lowered during the attack.

The advantage to implementing the WFQ mechanism is not only its relative simplicity, but also its effectiveness in preventing degradation of voice services during targeted SMS attacks. Unfortunately, the granularity for prioritizing text messages is insufficient to provide adequate service to those users relying upon text messaging as their dominant means of communication. Accordingly, if users believe that their traffic is unlikely to be delivered, their faith in text messaging as a reliable service will decrease. While finer granularity can be provided by adding one queue per SMS class, this solution will result in inefficient memory use and complexity. We discuss means of adding such granularity through the use of WRED.

5.9.2 Weighted Random Early Detection

Analysis

Active queue management has received a great deal of attention as a congestion avoidance mechanism in the Internet. *Random Early Detection* (RED) [71, 44], one of the better known techniques from this field, is a particularly effective means of coping with potentially damaging quantities of text messages. While traditionally used to address TCP congestion, RED helps to prevent queue lockout and RED drops packets arriving to a queue with a probability that is a function of the weighted queue occupancy average, Q_{avg}. Packets arriving to a queue capacity below a threshold, t_{min}, are never dropped. Packets arriving to a queue capacity above some value t_{max} are always dropped. Between t_{min} and t_{max}, packets are dropped with a linearly increasing probability up to $P_{drop,max}$. This probability, P_{drop}, is calculated as follows[14]:

$$P_{drop} = P_{drop,max} \cdot (Q_{avg} - t_{min})/(t_{max} - t_{min}) \qquad (5.1)$$

The advantages to this approach are twofold: first, lockout becomes more difficult as packets are purposefully dropped with greater frequency; secondly, because the capacity of busy queues stays closer to a moving average and not capacity, space typically exists to accommodate sudden bursts of traffic. However, one of the chief difficulties with traditional RED is that it eliminates the ability of a provider to offer QoS guarantees because all traffic entering a queue is dropped with equal probability. *Weighted Random Early Detection* (WRED) solves this problem by basing the probability a given incoming message is dropped on an attribute such as its contents, source or destination. Arriving messages not meeting some priority are therefore subject to increased probability of drop. The dropping probability for each class of message is tuned by setting $t_{priority,min}$ and $t_{priority,max}$ for each class.

We consider the use of authentication as a means of creating messaging priority classes. For example, during a crisis, messages injected to a network from the Internet by an authenticated municipality or from emergency personnel could receive priority over all other text messages. A number of municipalities already use such systems for emergency [155] and traffic updates [170]. Messages from authenticated users within the network itself receive secondary priority. Unauthenticated messages originating from the Internet are delivered

---

[14] Some variants of RED additionally incorporate a *count* variable. Equation 5.1 is the simplest version of RED defined by RFC 2309 [44].

with the lowest priority. Such a system would allow the informative messages (i.e., evacuation plans, additional warnings) to be quickly distributed amongst the population. The remaining messages would then be delivered at ratios corresponding to their priority level. We assume that packet priority marking occurs at the SMSCs such that additional computational burden is not placed on base stations.

Here, we illustrate how WRED can provide differentiated service to different classes of SMS traffic using the attack scenario described in Tables 5.3 and 5.4. We maintain separate queues, which are served in a round robin fashion, for voice requests and SMS requests. We apply WRED to the SMS queue. We assume legitimate text messages arrive at a sector with an average rate of 0.7 $msgs/sec$ with the following distribution: 10% high priority, 80% medium priority, and 10% low priority. The attack generates an additional 9 $msgs/sec$.

To accommodate sudden bursts of high priority SMS traffic, we choose an SMS queue size of 12. Because we desire low latency delivery of high priority messages, we target an average queue occupancy $Q_{avg} = 3$.

To meet this objective, we must set $t_{low,min}$ and $t_{low,max}$. For M/M/n systems with a finite queue of size m, the number of messages in the queue, N_Q, is:

$$N_Q = P_Q \frac{\rho}{1 - \rho} \tag{5.2}$$

where:

$$P_Q = \frac{p_0 (m\rho)^m}{m!(1 - \rho)} \tag{5.3}$$

where:

$$p_0 = \left[\sum_{n=0}^{m-1} \frac{(m\rho)^n}{n!} + \frac{(m\rho)^m}{m!(1 - \rho)} \right]^{-1} \tag{5.4}$$

Setting $N_Q = 3$, we derive a target load $\rho_{target} = 0.855$. ρ_{target} is the utilization desired at the SDCCHs. Thus, the packet dropping caused by WRED must reduce the actual utilization, ρ_{actual} or $\lambda_{SMS}/(\mu_{SMS} \cdot n)$, caused by the heavy offered load during an attack, to ρ_{target}. Therefore:

$$\rho_{target} = \rho_{actual}(1 - P_{drop}) \tag{5.5}$$

where P_{drop} is the overall dropping probability of WRED. For traffic with average arrival rate of $\lambda_{SMS} = 9.7$ $msgs/sec$, $\rho_{actual} = 3.23$. Solving for P_{drop},

$$P_{drop} = 1 - \frac{\rho_{target}}{\rho_{actual}} = 0.736 \tag{5.6}$$

P_{drop} can be calculated from the dropping probabilities of the individual classes of messages by ($\lambda_{low} = 9.07$):

$$P_{drop} = \frac{P_{drop,high} \cdot \lambda_{high} + P_{drop,med} \cdot \lambda_{med} + P_{drop,low} \cdot \lambda_{low}}{\lambda_{SMS}} \tag{5.7}$$

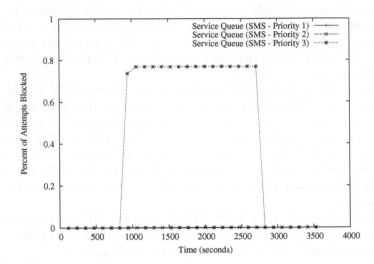

Fig. 5.14. The simulated blocking probability for a sector implementing WRED. Unlike WFQ, only Internet-originated text messages are dropped at an elevated frequency.

Because we desire to deliver all messages of high and medium priority, we set $P_{drop,high} = P_{drop,med} = 0$. Using Equation 5.7, we find $P_{drop,low} = 0.787$. This value is then used in conjunction with Equation 5.1 to determine $t_{low,min}$ and $t_{low,max}$.

The desired average queue occupancy, Q_{avg}, is 3. From equation 5.1, $t_{low,min}$ must be an integer less than the average queue occupancy. This leaves three possible values for $t_{low,min}$: 0, 1, and 2. The best fit is found when $t_{low,min} = 0$ and $t_{low,max} = 4$, resulting in 75% dropping of low priority traffic.

Using this method it is possible to set thresholds to meet delivery targets. Of course, depending on the intensity of an attack, it may not be possible to meet desired targets according to Equation 5.7, i.e., it may not be possible to limit blocking to only low priority traffic. While the method outlined here provides just an approximate solution, given the quantization error in setting $t_{low,min}$ and $t_{low,max}$ (they must be integers), we believe the method is sufficient.

Simulation

The use of a prioritized dropping policy allows a system to offer similar prioritization to WFQ while maintaining only a single queue. In our implementation of WRED, we maintain one queue for voice requests (size of 6) and one queue for SMS messages (size 12) and apply WRED to the SMS queue. We differentiate the SMS traffic by setting different thresholds for each class. We

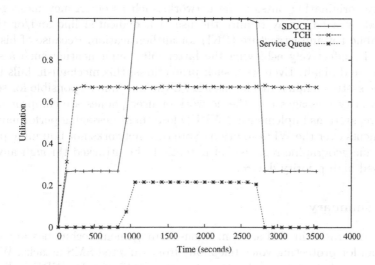

Fig. 5.15. Utilization for a sector implementing WRED. Note that the queue occupancy is low due to the decreased priority of Internet-originated messages.

assume that SMS traffic is marked upstream as having high, medium, or low priority. We assign the thresholds as $(t_{high,max} = t_{high,min} = 12)$, medium $(t_{med,max} = 10, t_{med,min} = 6)$ and low $(t_{low,max} = 4, t_{low,min} = 0)$ priority. These priorities correspond directly to emergency priority users, network customers and Internet-originated messages, respectively. Q_{avg} is maintained as a simple weighted average with a weight of 0.8 on the most recent sample.

Figure 5.14 gives the blocking for each of the three priorities of text messages. Because voice calls never block in these simulations, we omit them from this graph. Both high and medium priority flows also do not experience blocking throughout the simulations. The blocking of Internet-originated messages averages 77%, approximately the same blocking probability experienced by all incoming messages in the base attack scenarios. Service queue utilization, shown in Figure 5.15, is 20%. With a total queue capacity of 18, this corresponds to an average occupancy of 3.88 messages. Also notice that the TCH occupancy is maintained throughout the attack.

The parameters used in this simulation are the same as those in Table 5.3. We set the medium priority thresholds to allow some loss at very high loads to protect the high priority traffic under extreme circumstances, but because our average queue occupancy is about 3.9, no dropping of medium priority messages occurs. This matches well with our analytical results.

Systems implementing WRED not only match the elimination of voice call blocking seen through the use of WFQ, but also offer significantly improved performance in terms of message delivery. Implementing this solution, however, faces its own challenges. The authentication of high priority messages, for example, would require the use of additional infrastructure. High priority messages originating outside the network, such as emergency messages distributed by a city, may require the use of a dedicated line and/or the use of a public key infrastructure (PKI) for authentication. Because of historical difficulties effectively achieving the latter [59], implementing such a system may prove difficult. Even with such protections, this mechanism fails to protect the system against insider attacks. If the machine responsible for sending high priority messages into the network or user phones are compromised by malware, systems implementing WRED lose their messaging performance improvements over the WFQ solution. Note that networks not bounding priority to specific geographic regions can potentially be attacked through any compromised high priority device.

5.9.3 Summary

As demonstrated in this section, queue management techniques are a valuable tool for protecting voice telephony from targeted SMS attacks. Whereas both approaches protect voice from targeted SMS attacks, WRED allows for greater classification of traffic without the significant added overhead WFQ would require to implement multiple queues. The benefits of these schemes, however, are more limited than in traditional data networks. For instance, the shedding of TCP packets in an IP network should cause flow control mechanisms to reduce transmission rates. Because the same does not happen here, queue management techniques essentially "bail water" until an attack subsides. Accordingly, such mechanisms should be relied upon as a last line of defense. We therefore look to techniques that reapportion the resources on the air interface for a more flexible response.

5.10 Resource Provisioning

None of the above methods deal with the system bottleneck directly; rather, they strive to affect traffic before it reaches the air interface. An alternative strategy of addressing targeted SMS attacks instead focuses on the reallocation of the available messaging bandwidth. We therefore investigate a variety of techniques that modify the way in which the air interface is used.

To analyze these techniques we resort to simple Erlang-B queuing analysis. We present a brief background here. For more details see Schwartz [162]. In a system with n servers, and an offered load in Erlangs of A, the probability that an arriving request is blocked because all servers are occupied is given by:

$$P_B = \frac{\frac{A^n}{n!}}{\sum_{l=0}^{l=n-1} \frac{Al}{l!}} \tag{5.8}$$

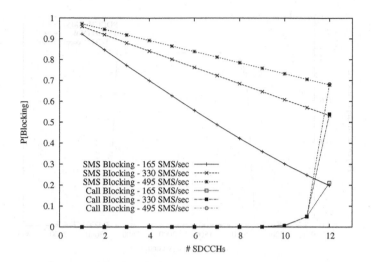

Fig. 5.16. The probability that incoming calls and SMS messages are blocked in a system implementing SRP. We vary the number of SDCCHs that will accept SMS requests from 1 to 12(all).

The load in Erlangs is the same as the utilization, ρ, in a queuing system; it is simply the offered load multiplied by the service time of the resource. The expected occupancy of the servers is given by:

$$E(n) = \rho(1 - P_B) \qquad (5.9)$$

5.10.1 Strict Resource Provisioning

Analysis

Under normal conditions, the resources for service setup and delivery are over-provisioned. At a rate of $50,000$ *calls/city/hour* in our baseline scenario, for example, the calculated average utilization of SDCCHs per sector is approximately 2%. Given this observation, if a subset of the total SDCCHs can be used only by voice calls, blocking due to targeted SMS attacks can be significantly mitigated. Our first air interface provisioning technique, *Strict Resource Provisioning* (SRP), attempts to address this contention by allowing text messages to occupy only a subset of the total number of SDCCHs in a sector. Requests for incoming voice calls can compete for the entire set of SDCCHs, including the subset used for SMS. In order to determine appropriate parameters for systems using SRP, we apply Equations 5.8 and 5.9.

To isolate the effectiveness of SRP, we consider a system with no queue. Figure 5.16 shows the blocking probabilities for a system using SRP when we

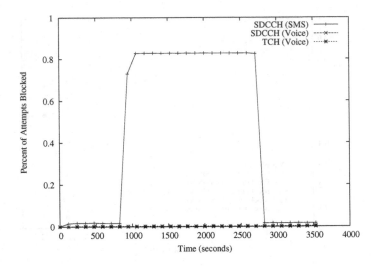

Fig. 5.17. Blocking for a sector implementing SRP

vary the number of SDCCHs that will accept SMS requests from 1 to 12 (all). Because incoming text messages only compete with voice calls for a subset of the resources, any resulting call blocking is strictly a function of the size of the subset of voice-only SDCCHs. The attacks of intensity 165, 330, and 495 *msgs/city/sec* (3, 6, and 9 messages/second/sector) have virtually no impact on voice calls until the full complement of SDCCHs are made available to all traffic. In fact, it is not until 10 SDCCHs are made available to SMS traffic that the blocking probability for incoming voice calls reaches 1%.

By limiting the number of SDCCHs that will serve SMS requests, the blocking for SMS is increased. When only six SDCCHs are available to text messages, blocking probabilities for SMS are as high as 84%. Because significant numbers of people rely upon text messaging as their primary means of communication, such parameters should be carefully tuned.

Simulation

Before characterizing the SRP technique, careful consideration was given to the selection of operating parameters. Because many MSCs are capable of processing up to 500K *calls/hour*, we engineer our solution to be robust to large spikes in traffic. We therefore allow SMS traffic to use 6 of the 12 total SDCCHs, which yields a blocking probability of 1% of voice calls by the SDCCH when voice traffic requests reach 250,000 *calls/hour*. (Note that calls would experience an average blocking probability of 71% due to a lack of TCHs with requests at this intensity.) Because these networks are designed to operate dependably during elevated traffic conditions, we believe that the above settings are realistic.

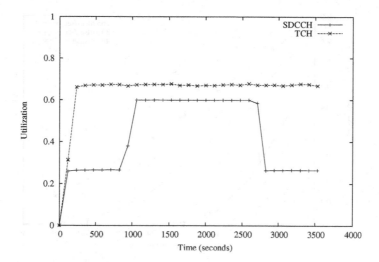

Fig. 5.18. Channel utilization under SRP

The blocking probabilities for SMS and voice flows in a sector implementing SRP are shown in Figure 5.17. Because SRP prevents text messages from competing for all possible SDCCHs, voice calls experience no blocking on the SDCCHs throughout the duration of the attack. Text messages, however, are blocked at a rate of 83%. Channel utilization, illustrated in Figure 5.18, gives additional insight into network conditions. Because calling behavior remains the same during the attack, the resources allocated by the network are more than sufficient to provide voice service to users. By design, SDCCH utilization plateaus well below full capacity. While the SDCCHs used by text messages have an average utilization of 97%, the SDCCHs used by incoming voice calls average a utilization of 6.3%. This under-use of resources represents a potential loss of utility as the majority of text messages (legitimate or otherwise) go undelivered.

The difficulty with this solution is correct parameter setting. While theoretical results indicate that allocating 10 SDCCHs only increases call blocking to 1%, voice traffic volumes fluctuate throughout the day. Provisioning resources in a static fashion must account for worst-case scenarios and therefore leads to conservative settings. While protecting the network from an attack, such a mechanism may actually hinder the efficiency of normal operation. When traffic channels are naturally saturated, as may be common during an emergency or elevated traffic scenario discussed in Section 5.6, such hard limits actually prevent users from communicating. Furthermore, as unsustained bursts of text messages are generally innocuous, such a limitation may directly impact the provider's ability to generate revenue as user perception of SMS

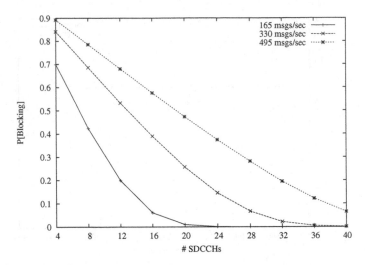

Fig. 5.19. The probability of an incoming call/message blocking in a sector for a varying number of SDCCHs.

as a real-time service erodes. Determining the correct balance between insulation from attacks and resource utilization becomes non-trivial. Accordingly, we look to our other techniques for more complete solutions.

5.10.2 Dynamic Resource Provisioning

Analysis

While SRP reprovisions capacity on existing SDCCHs, other over-provisioned resources in the sector could be manipulated to alleviate SDCCH congestion. For example, at a rate of 50,000 *calls/hour*, each sector uses an average of 67% of its TCHs. If a small number of unused TCHs could be repurposed as SDCCHs, additional bandwidth could be provided to mitigate such attacks.

Our second air interface technique, *Dynamic Resource Provisioning* (DRP), attempts to mitigate targeted text messaging attacks by temporarily reclaiming a number of TCHs (up to some limit) for use as SDCCHs. This approach is highly practical for a number of reasons. First, increasing the bandwidth (762 bits/second) of individual SDCCHs is difficult without making significant changes to either the radio encoding or the architecture of the air interface itself. Because major changes to the network are extremely expensive and typically occur over the course of many years, such fixes are not appropriate in the short term. Secondly, dynamically reclaiming channels allows the network to adjust itself to current conditions. During busy hours such as morning and evening commutes, for example, channels temporarily used as SDCCHs can

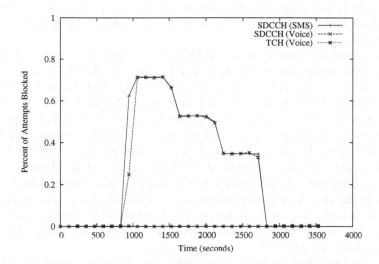

Fig. 5.20. Blocking for a sector implementing DRP

be returned to the pool of TCHs to accommodate elevated voice traffic needs. Lastly, because SDCCHs are assigned via the AGCH, allocating incoming requests to seemingly random timeslots requires almost no changes to handset software.

Figure 5.19 demonstrates the blocking probability for incoming calls and text messages in a sector using DRP to add a variable number of SDCCHs. Again, no queue was used. The ability of an attacker to block all channels is significantly reduced as the number of SDCCHs increases. Attackers are therefore forced to increase the intensity of their attack in order to maintain its potency. For attacks at a rate of 165 $msgs/sec$, doubling the number of available SDCCHs reduces the calculated blocking caused by an attack by two orders of magnitude. The blocking probability caused by attacks at higher rates, in which the number of Erlangs is greater than the number of SDCCHs, decreases in roughly a linear relationship to the number of SDCCHs added.

One potential drawback with DRP is that by subtracting TCHs from the system, it is possible to increase call blocking because of TCH exhaustion. In fact, the reclamation of TCHs for use as SDCCHs increases the blocking probability for voice calls from 0.2% in the base scenario (45 TCHs, 12 SDCCHs) to 1.5% where 40 SDCCHs are available (a reduction to 40 TCHs).

Simulation

Although it is possible to reclaim any number of TCHs for use as SDCCHs under the DRP mechanism, we limited the candidate number of channels for this conversion to two. In these experiments, a single TCH was repurposed into 8 SDCCHs every 10 minutes during the attack. This separation was designed to allow the network to return to steady state between channel allocations. While converting only two channels is not enough to completely eliminate attacks at high intensities, our goal is to understand the behavior of this mechanism.

The blocking probabilities for SMS and voice flows in a sector implementing the DRP technique are illustrated in Figure 5.20. As TCHs are converted for use as SDCCHs, the blocking probabilities for both incoming SMS and voice requests fall from 72% to 53% and eventually 35%. This represents a total reduction of the blocking probability by approximately half. Call blocking due to TCH exhaustion was not observed despite the reduced number of available TCHs. Figure 5.21 illustrates a gradual return towards pre-attack TCH utilization levels as additional SDCCHs are allocated. The effects of the reprovisioning are also obvious for SDCCH utilization. The downward spikes represent the sudden influx of additional, temporarily unused channels. While SDCCH utilization quickly returns to nearly identical levels after each reallocation, more voice calls can be completed due to a decrease probability of the attack holding all SDCCHs at any given time.

As was a problem for SRP, determining the correct parameters for DRP is a difficult undertaking. The selection of two TCHs for conversion to SDCCHs illustrates the utility of this mechanism, but is not sufficient for real settings. To reduce the blocking probability on SDCCHs below the values observed for TCHs, a total of 48 SDCCHs would have to be made available. This leaves 39 TCHs, which results in a call blocking probability of 2.1% due to TCH exhaustion. Elevations in the volume of voice calls would likely require the release of some number of reclaimed TCHs to be repurposed to their original use.

The decision to convert channels is also non-trivial. Whereas the decision to reallocate channels at specific times was decided statically in our simulation, dynamically determining these parameters would prove significantly more challenging. Basing reclamation decisions on small observation windows, while offering greater responsiveness, may result in decreased resource use due to thrashing. If the observation window becomes too large, an attack may end before appropriate action can be taken. As was observed for SRP, the static allocation of additional SDCCHs faces similar inflexibility problems. Low resource utilization under normal operating conditions again represents a potential loss of opportunity and revenue.

5.10.3 Direct Channel Allocation

Analysis

From the security perspective, the ideal means of eliminating the competition for resources between call setup and SMS delivery would be through the separation of shared mechanisms. Specifically, delivering text messages and incoming call requests over mutually exclusive sets of channels would prevent

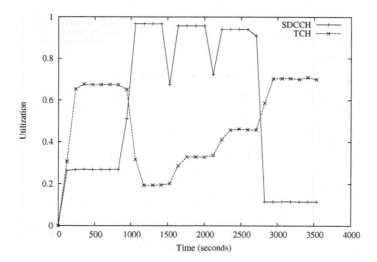

Fig. 5.21. Channel utilization under DRP

these flows from interfering with each other. The challenge of implementing such a mechanism is to do so without requiring significant restructuring
of the network architecture or incurring tremendous expense. As previously
mentioned, such fundamental changes in network operation are typically too
expensive and time consuming to be considered in the short term. While the
SRP technique provides a rudimentary separation, it is possible to further
isolate these two types of traffic.

As mentioned in the previous section, DRP is easily implementable because
the AGCH specifies the location of the SDCCH allocated for a specific session.
After call requests finish using their assigned SDCCH, they are instructed to
listen to a specific TCH. Because the use of a TCH is the eventual goal of
incoming voice calls, it is therefore possible to shortcut the use of SDCCHs
for call setup. Incoming calls could therefore be directed to a TCH, leaving
SDCCHs exclusively for the delivery of SMS messages. This technique, which
we refer to as *Direct Channel Allocation* (DCA), removes the shared SDCCH
channels as the system bottleneck.

Calculating blocking probabilities for a system implementing DCA is a
matter of analyzing SDCCH and TCH blocking for the two independent flows.
For 165 *msgs/sec*, text messages have a calculated blocking probability of approximately 20%. This value increases to 68% as the attack intensity increases
to 495 *msgs/sec*. Voice calls, at an average rate of 50,000 *calls/hour*, have
a blocking probability of 0.2%. Note that because the shared bottleneck has
been removed, it becomes extremely difficult for targeted text messaging attacks to have any effect on voice communications.

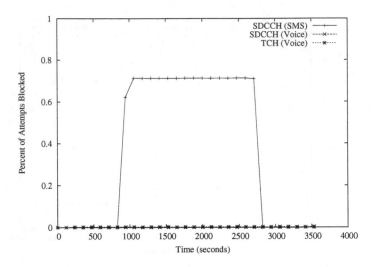

Fig. 5.22. Blocking for a sector implementing DCA

Simulation

To simulate the DCA mechanism, incoming voice calls skip directly from the RACH to the next available TCH. An average of 1.5 additional seconds was added to each incoming call duration to account for the processing formerly occurring on an SDCCH. As is shown in Figure 5.22, voice calls arriving in a sector implementing the DCA scheme experience no additional blocking during a targeted SMS attack. Figure 5.23 confirms the results in the previous figure by showing the constant TCH utilization throughout the duration of the attack. No additional assistance is provided for the delivery of text messages under DCA.

While removing the bottleneck on the shared path of SMS delivery and voice call setup, DCA potentially introduces new vulnerabilities into the network. One advantage of using SDCCHs to perform call establishment is that users are authenticated before they are assigned TCHs. Under the DCA model, however, valuable traffic channels can be occupied before users are ever authenticated. Using a single phone planted in a targeted area, an attacker could simply respond to all paging messages and then ignore all future communications from the network. Because there are legitimate reasons to wait tens of seconds for a phone to reply to a page, an attacker could force the network to open and maintain state for multiple connections that would eventually go unused. Note that because paging for individual phones occurs over multiple sectors, a single rogue phone could quickly create a black-hole effect. Such an attack is very similar to the classic SYN attack observed throughout the Inter-

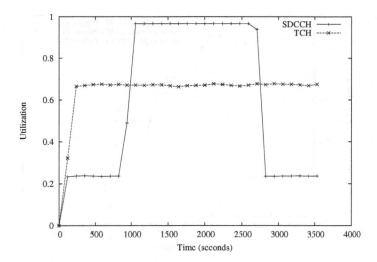

Fig. 5.23. Channel utilization under DCA

net. While seemingly the most complete, the potential for additional damage made possible because of the DCA approach should be carefully considered.

5.10.4 Summary

The resource management techniques presented above offer a number of valuable countermeasures against targeted SMS attacks. At a high level, SRP provides functionality to the weighted fair queuing approach under high load by ensuring that channels are always available to voice traffic. SRP, however, experiences even high rates of SMS blocking than weighted fair queuing (83% vs 72%). DRP allows the network to accommodate spikes in traffic by reapportioning unused TCHs, thereby making the network more flexible to a wider range of operating conditions. As we discovered in the DCA case, however, the repurposing of resources must be carefully executed so as to not introduce new vulnerabilities into the system.

5.11 Combining Mechanisms

There is no "silver-bullet" for maintaining a high quality of service for both text messaging and voice calls during a targeted SMS attack. As the above techniques demonstrate, each potential solution has its own weaknesses. The combination of such solutions, however, offers techniques robust to a wider array of threats. We examine two examples in which the fusion of mechanisms provides additional protections.

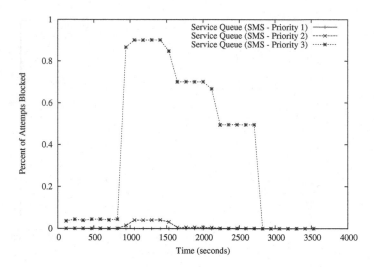

Fig. 5.24. Blocking for a sector implementing both WRED and DRP.

While directly addressing the bandwidth issue that makes targeted SMS attacks possible, the DRP technique lacks granularity to separate incoming voice and SMS requests. WRED, on the other hand, provides such traffic classification but is unable to react to attacks originating from trusted sources. To illustrate the benefits of layering these techniques, we increase the volume of legitimate traffic to 2 $msgs/sector/sec$, with 90% of that traffic being medium priority and the remaining 10% split equally between high and low priority flows. Such an increase would be representative of the elevated volumes of messages sent from crowded events such as concerts or public celebrations such as New Year's Eve gatherings. Figure 5.24 shows the result of the combination of the two techniques during an attack. Because of the naturally increased volume of legitimate traffic, subscriber-to-subscriber traffic experiences approximately 5% blocking in a sector only implementing WRED. As DRP activates and adds additional SDCCHs, only the attack traffic is dropped. Such a technique may be especially valuable during an emergency, as additional bandwidth can be provisioned to clients less likely to be malicious.

Another potentially beneficial combination is SRP and DRP. Given high volumes of voice traffic, a provider may not be able to repurpose enough SDCCHs to eliminate the effects of a targeted text messaging attack. Instead, a subset of the total channels could be reserved for voice requests. In so doing, voice blocking due to targeted text messaging attacks could be eliminated. All additional channels could be added to reduce blocking for text messages. Figure 5.25 illustrates an attack scenario in which two TCHs are reclaimed for use as SDCCHs, with 18 of 24 total SDCCHs made available to SMS. Note

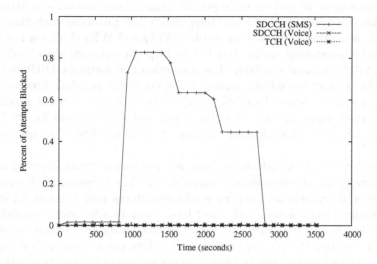

Fig. 5.25. Blocking for a sector combining DRP and SRP.

both the elimination of call blocking and the gradual reduction of blocking rates for text messages.

Other combinations are less useful. Integrating WRED and SRP, for example, would simply reduce the bandwidth made available for even high priority mechanisms. Accordingly, the network may experience decreased throughput for legitimate messages than under either scheme alone. The use of DCA with any other mechanism fails to prevent the vulnerability introduced in the previous subsection, and therefore does not warrant further investigation.

While no susceptible examples were uncovered during the course of this research, the combination of any of the above mitigation techniques should also be carefully considered. This fusion may lead to the creation of new or magnification of previously mentioned vulnerabilities. Accordingly, additional testing on development networks should be conducted before such integration could occur.

5.12 Summary

For targets ranging from individuals and metropolitan areas to entire countries, targeted text messaging attacks are capable of causing serious disruptions to service. As our modeling and simulation illustrate, an adversary with the bandwidth available to a cable modem is capable of denying service to over 70% of calls in Manhattan. We then show that currently available "edge solutions" fail to consider all possible attack vectors.

Our focus then shifted to mitigation through a number of techniques from queue management and resource provisioning. These mechanisms attempt to maintain the availability of voice telephony while providing high throughput for text messaging with varying results. WFQ and WRED offer a last line of defense by separating traffic, but fail to help the network absorb additional traffic. SRP functions similarly. The remaining two methods, DRP and DCA, allow the network to dedicate unused resources to the problem; however, DCA creates a serious new vulnerability and is therefore not a viable solution. In spite of these shortcomings, all of the above techniques except for DCA offers an effective means of mitigating the impact of targeted SMS attacks on voice calls.

The attacks discussed throughout are representative of growing and increasingly problematic class of vulnerabilities. The connectivity between the Internet and traditional voice networks introduces new avenues for exploit: once confined to exploiting only inert hosts, remote adversaries can debilitate the services we depend on to carry on our daily lives. In a broader sense, the ability to control the physical world via the Internet is inherently dangerous, and more so when the affected components are part of critical infrastructure. This work provides some preliminary solutions and analysis for these vulnerabilities. Essential future work will seek more general solutions that address these vulnerabilities in current and next generation networks.

6

Vulnerabilities in Cellular Data Networks

The modest capabilities of mobile devices have long limited the services provided by the telecommunications infrastructure to telephony. As many of these limitations have been overcome, the desire for such devices to interact with the larger Internet has increase. In response, cellular providers now offer a high-speed data services such as the General Packet Data Service (GPRS). While greatly extending the connectivity of mobile users, the interconnection of the telecommunications infrastructure with data traffic and the larger Internet significantly increases the attack surface of these systems.

In this chapter, we examine vulnerabilities in high-speed cellular data services. We begin by discussing the history and evolution of cellular data services. We then present a thorough description of packet delivery, including the processes associated with device setup. These descriptions set the stage for attacks on connection establishment and teardown mechanisms. Modeling and simulation show that an adversary can cause blocking for greater than 96% of data requests for high-speed cellular data services with only 160kbps of attack traffic. This volume represents approximately one-third of the traffic used to deny service to the lower bandwidth Short Messaging Service in Chapter 5. We then show how the sharing of connection setup mechanisms allows such attacks to impact voice services in the network. We then examine ways in which such attacks could be mitigated.

This Chapter asks a larger question: *"How does the architecture of cellular data networks inherently make them susceptible to denial of service attacks?"* Unexpectedly, the answer to this question has little to do with bandwidth constraints. Instead, these vulnerabilities are the result of the conflict caused by connecting two networks built on fundamentally opposing design philosophies. We argue that low-bandwidth denial of service attacks in telecommunications networks are artifacts of incompatibility caused by interconnecting systems built with two differing sets of design requirements. While the merits of independent "smart" and "dumb" architectures have been widely debated, none have examined the inherent security issues caused by the connection of two mature systems built on these opposing design tenets. Through this, we seek

to develop a larger sense for *why* such attacks are possible, even in the presence
of a cellular network with hypothetically infinite bandwidth. Ultimately, by
understanding causality, the discovery of future vulnerabilities is vastly simplified. We note that this is only a start in understanding the vulnerabilities
present in cellular data services.

6.1 History and Description

Data services have been available from cellular networks for a number of
years. Users could use their phones as a dial-up connection to their ISP.
As discussed in Chapter 3, however, the voice encoding mechanism in GSM
limited maximum bandwidth because of it is optimized to compress human
voices. Standards documents go as far as to note that " [t]ests have shown
that voice-band transmission does not work satisfactorily with 1200 bit/s
modems" [10]. In response to growing demand for services supporting mod-
erate bandwidth, providers introduced new encoding methods for data-only
calls. *Circuit Switched Data* (CSD), which significantly improved its encoding
over previous analog data services, provided users with rates as theoretically
high as 9.6kbps [1] using a single GSM timeslot. Further demand for improved
access speeds brought about the creation of the *High Speed Circuit Switched
Data* (HSCSD) service, which enhance end-user bandwidth to as much as
38.4kbps by allocating as many as four CSD timeslots per user.

Like voice telephony, these circuit-switched services require that a single
endpoint monopolize a channel for the entire duration of its connection to the
network. As a side-effect, cellular networks had the potential to offer quality
of service guarantees to their customers. Such guarantees come at a price to
users. Regardless of whether this connection was used to constantly stream
content or intermittently deliver packets, the provider charged the end user for
the entire duration of the connection. Accordingly, demand for such inefficient
services has not been great.

GPRS overcomes these limitations by multiplexing multiple traffic flows
over individual links. Accordingly, it is possible to serve a large number of users
on a single physical channel concurrently and only charge them for the packets
they exchange. As described in detail in Chapter 3, packets in GPRS networks
can be transmitted using one of four coding schemes (CS-1 to CS-4) [21].
This results in maximum download rates ranging from 9kbps to 21.4kbps per
timeslot. *Enhanced Data rates for GSM Evolution* (EDGE), also known as
Enhanced GPRS (EGPRS), improves the performance of GPRS by replacing
the coding scheme with the higher-bandwidth *8-Phase Shift Keying* (8PSK).

---

[1] The maximum speed of CSD channels depend on the transmission frequency
of the network. The most widely used networks, GSM-900MHz, can achieve a
theoretical maximum of 9.6kbps. Less widespread GSM-1800MHz networks can
reach a theoretical maximum of 14.4kbps. Our discussion assumes GSM-900MHz.

8PSK increases bandwidth per timeslot to as high as 59.2kbps [14]. Available bandwidth in either of the above two systems can be further improved by allowing mobile devices to listen to multiple timeslots.

While their adoption is still not universal, the use and availability of packet-switched cellular data services far exceeds that of circuit-switched services. Because the wide range of requirements for real-time data applications are unlikely to supported soley by packet-switched services, standards documents for third generation data networks such as UMTS continue to provide both support for both options.

6.2 Delivering Packets from the Internet

6.2.1 Device Registration

Before a GPRS/EDGE network provides any services to a mobile device user, a series of attachment and authentication procedures must take place. On power-up, a device (e.g., mobile phone) transmits a *GPRS-attach* message to the network. The base station forwards this message to the attached *Serving GPRS Support Node* (SGSN), which authenticates the user's identity with the help of the *Home Location Register* (HLR). The HLR supports both voice and data operations in the network by keeping track of information including user location, availability and accessible services. When this process completes, the mobile device has a virtual connection with the network.

Device registration with the voice and data elements of the network need not be mutually exclusive events. In order to reduce the resources used during registration, networks provide for a combined IMSI/GPRS attach procedure. Before sending an *Attach Accept* message to device performing registration, the SGSN creates an association between itself and the MSC/VLR corresponding to the device by sending a *Base Station System Application Part +* (BSSAP+) message. The identity of the MSC/VLR is determined by translating the device's *Routing Area Identity* (RAI) into a VLR number. When such an association is made, the network then forwards all incoming call requests to the SGSN in order to coordinate all paging activities from a single network element [13]. The details of combined paging are provided in Section 6.2.4.

In order to exchange packets with external networks, the mobile device must then establish a *Packet Data Protocol* (PDP) context with the network. The PDP context is a data structure stored in the SGSN and the *Gateway GPRS Support Node* (GGSN) and is responsible for mapping billing information, quality of service requirements and an IP address to a user device. Mobile devices that have not initiated or have deactivated a PDP context are said to be in the INACTIVE state. Logically, when a device has established and continues to maintain a PDP context with the network, it is said to be in the ACTIVE state. PDP contexts themselves can be assigned both statically or dynamically, and devices can potentially support multiple PDP contexts concurrently. PDP context establishment may also be initiated by the network. If static PDP contexts are used and incoming packets are being queued, the network can begin the registration process on behalf of the targeted mobile device. The network can also modify parameters during of active PDP contexts (e.g., renegotiating QoS).

While many phones do not currently automatically establish a PDP context on power-up, the trend towards doing so is rapidly increasing. Many providers are also beginning to offer static IP addresses. As cellular providers move into the broadband Internet market, such numbers will continue to expand rapidly.

6.2.2 Submitting Packets

While not yet as popular as text messaging, cellular data services are seeing increased usage. Accordingly, providers are investigating new methods of encouraging service uptake. Like SMS, this includes supporting portals and applications linking the telecommunications infrastructure with the Internet. Verizon Wireless, for instance, provides an open interface on their website allowing users to send MMS messages to subscriber phones [189]. In addition to offering a selection of images, this interface also allows the sender to upload files to a subscriber device. Both Verizon and AT&T Wireless [35] allow anyone to send MMS messages via email to their subscribers.

The diversity of devices now capable of connecting to the Internet through cellular networks ever growing. In addition to the limited access associated with traditional mobile phones through interfaces such as WAP, more capable smart phones and even laptops can now connect to the Internet via services such as GPRS. PCMCIA cards even allow the potential for desktop PCs to receive broadband access wirelessly.

All of these new devices and services represent new connections between the telecommunications infrastructure and the Internet. Whether via asynchronous (MMS, email) or synchronous (direct exchange of IP packets) means, the number of attack vectors targeting cellular data services are only increasing. As attackers are able to compromise mobile devices within provider networks, the source of attacks will no longer be limited to interactions with external networks. As discussed in Chapter 5, the ability to prevent such attacks using edge solutions will become increasingly inadequate as the connections between cellular networks and the Internet increase.

6.2.3 Routing Packets

Having been authenticated and registered, a mobile device is capable of exchanging packets with hosts internal and external to the cellular network. At some time after attachment, a packet originating from an Internet-based host and destined for a mobile device arrives at the GGSN. The GGSN compares the destination IP address to those of established PDP contexts and,

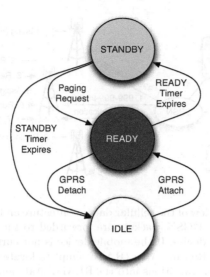

Fig. 6.1. A state transition diagram for mobile devices, including transition functions.

upon finding the corresponding entry, forwards the packet to the corresponding SGSN. As discussed in Chapter 3, each IP packet is tunneled between the GGSN and SGSN using *GPRS Tunneling Protocol* (GTP) over TCP or UDP [13]. While MAPsec or IPsec have been proposed to protect the confidentiality and integrity of messages as they traverse these networks, the deployment of both of these schemes is limited at best. Accordingly, source and destination nodes should not rely upon the network itself to ensure the confidentiality and integrity of their messages.

Upon arrival, the SGSN then begins the process of connection establishment and wireless delivery. Figure 6.2 highlights this network architecture.

6.2.4 Wireless Delivery

The final hop of packet delivery occurs over the air interface. The details of this step, however, depend upon the current state of the device. As power has traditionally been a concern in this setting, mobile devices are not constantly listening for incoming packets. To accommodate this constraint, devices operate in one of three states: IDLE, STANDBY, and READY. Devices in the IDLE state are unregistered with the network and therefore unreachable. In the power-saving STANDBY state, in which the vast majority of time is spent, devices periodically listen for network "wake up" messages known as pages. To preserve the anonymity of mobile users from eavesdroppers, paging messages contain a *Packet Temporary Mobile Subscriber Identifier* (P-TMSI), which is functionally equivalent to the TMSI discussed previously. Upon receiving a page from the network, the device transitions into the READY state. In this

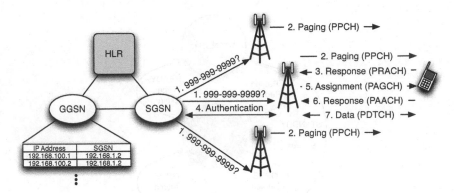

Fig. 6.2. A high level view of the cellular data architecture and packet delivery. After being looked up in the GGSN, packets are forwarded to the SGSN corresponding to the targeted mobile device. If the mobile device is not currently in the READY state, all towers in the Routing Area (RA) attempt to locate the device. When the device responds, it then transitions into the READY state and establishes a virtual connection over the wireless interface.

state, a device constantly monitors the air interface for incoming packets. When packets are not received for a number of seconds, devices transition back into the STANDBY state to conserve power. These three states and the transitions between them are shown in Figure 6.1. Note that a PDP context (i.e., a transition between the INACTIVE and ACTIVE PDP context states) can only occur when a device is in STANDBY or READY modes.

On the arrival of the first packet in a flow, the SGSN begins the process of locating the targeted device. If the destination device is not currently in the READY state, the base station nearest to the device is unknown to the network. Accordingly, the SGSN creates paging messages to be sent from a number of base stations. Upon receiving a paging request, a base station transmits a message to multiple sectors (i.e., service areas) over the *Packet Paging Channel* (PPCH). Whether due to interference or sleep cycles, the paging process typically requires multiple iterations. If the targeted device is awake and hears its temporary identifier in a paging message, it attempts to alert the network of its presence by responding on the *Packet Random Access Channel* (PRACH). The base station receiving this response alerts the SGSN that the destination device has been located. The network then responds on the *Packet Access Grant Channel* (PAGCH) with a message containing a list of *Packet Data Traffic Channels* (PDTCHs) that should be monitored for incoming data. The device acknowledges receiving this message over the *Packet Associated Control Channel* (PACCH). At the end of this setup, as illustrated in Figure 6.2, the network can then route traffic directly to the READY state device. Note that the above channels are largely complementary to channels used for voice signaling (the naming convention, minus the "Packet" prefix, is the same).

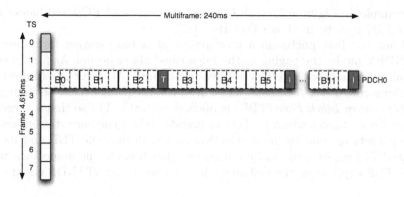

Fig. 6.3. Each timeslot in a GPRS TDMA frame is used to create physical channels called Packet Data Channels (PDCHs). Every 52-frame set forms a multiframe, which itself is divided into 12 bursts of 4 timeslots. Each group, or burst, holds a single logical channel. The specific allocation of these channels is dependent on the network and system load. The remaining timeslots are used for time synchronization (T) and network measurement (I).

Paging and setup for both circuit-switched (voice) and packet-switched (data) services can be coordinated. Because running two sets of control channels leads to the underuse of limited spectrum, the standards documents indicate that it is acceptable for voice and data control channels to be shared [13, 12, 22]. Such an optimization is also helpful from the perspective of mobile devices, which would be required to expend more energy listening to multiple control channels. We refer the reader to Section 6.4.1

6.3 Packet Multiplexing

GPRS provides data service by building on the timeslot structure of GSM. Specifically, a contiguous piece of radio spectrum is subdivided into equal timeslots. When assigned a timeslot, a user exerts temporary control over a small piece of the air interface. To provide the illusion of continuous control, sets of eight timeslots are grouped into a frame so that each can be serviced once every 4.615ms. This sampling across timeslots creates physical channels, upon which voice, data and control traffic can be delivered. When used for data, these physical channels are referred to as *Packet Data Channels* (PD-CHs). Each set of 52 frames creates larger units known as multiframes. These multiframes are subdivided into 12, four-timeslot blocks, with logical channels then mapped onto each block. The remaining four timeslots in a multiframe are used for time synchronization and signal strength measurement periods.

For example, in Figure 6.3, block $B0$ may function as a PPCH and blocks $B1$, $B4$ and $B7$ may be used as PDTCHs [2] [22].

When the first packet in a flow arrives at a base station for a user in STANDBY mode, the paging method described above occurs. As part of connection establishment, the flow receives a unique MAC layer label known as the *Temporary Flow Identifier* (TFI). Every subsequent packet belonging to the *Temporary Block Flow* (TBF) is marked with this TFI so that a targeted mobile device knows which packets to decode. When the base station has no more packets to send to the destination mobile device, the TBF and its associated TFI expire and can be reused by other flows in the immediate area. Upon TBF expiration, the mobile device returns to the STANDBY state.

6.4 Exploiting Cellular Data Services

6.4.1 Determining Network Settings

While the above descriptions offer significant information about cellular networks, they fail to provide many crucial operational details. For instance, the standards documents provide a range of options and configurations that providers can use to run their networks. Knowing which optimizations and settings are in effect has a significant impact on our ability to understand the impact of an adversary. Such information is, of course, closely guarded and not generally offered to the public.

Fortunately, as discussed in Chapter 5, there are methods of determining such unpublished settings. While our previous techniques relied on gray-box testing, more direct techniques are also applicable. Most mobile phones, for example, come equipped with additional software designed to provide supplementary information about the network. "Field Test" or "Engineering" Mode, as it is typically called, provides data ranging from the identity and signal strength of nearby towers to the layout of specific channels. For instance, the number of SDCCHs allotted in a given sector can be discovered in this mode of operation. More relevant to this particular work is the absence of a *Packet Broadcast Control Channel* (PBCCH), as shown by the PBCCH Present FALSE field in Figure 6.4. Such a revelation means that resources for paging and setup are in fact shared in some operational networks. Such information is included where possible in the simulations and discussions below. Other information is not ascertainable from Field Test Mode. Accordingly, our calculations and simulations remain conservative throughout the following sections.

Access to Field Test Mode does not allow an adversary to cause damage to a network. In spite of this, the use of this mode is generally restricted or

---

[2] Note the subtle difference in naming. PDTCHs are virtual channels that are run on top of physical PDCHs.

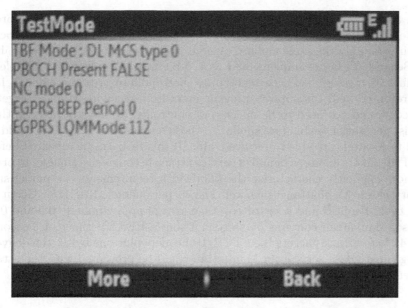

Fig. 6.4. A Samsun Blackjack (SGH-i607) running in Field Test Mode on the Cingular Wireless network. This mode of operation allows the device owner to learn information about the network including signal strength from surrounding towers and channel configuration.

hidden from most users. Lists of key sequences and custom builds of firmware supporting Field Test Mode are readily available throughout the Internet; however, use of such software may potentially irrevocably damage a user's phone and should be done only with extreme caution.

6.4.2 Exploiting Teardown Mechanisms

Analysis

Because the process of locating, paging and establishing a connection between the network and an end device is expensive, the immediate expiration of a TBF is impractical. For example, minor variations in packet interarrival times would force a system as described above to frequently relocate, repage and reestablish connectivity with users. Accordingly, networks implement a delayed teardown of resources. This means that devices remain in the READY state and retain their TBF for a number of seconds before the network attempts to reclaim its logical resources. When a packet is delivered to the user, the network sets a timer[3], which is reset to its default value on the arrival of

---

[3] This timer is referred to in the specifications as T3169 [11]. It is actually started when the counter N3101, which indicates the number of radio blocks that have

each additional packet. The standards recommend a timer value of approximately five seconds [11]. Given that the connection establishment process requires roughly the same amount of time, such a value is entirely reasonable.

Because TFIs are implemented as a 5-bit field, an adversary capable of sending 32 messages to each sector in a metropolitan area can exhaust logical resources and temporarily prevent users from receiving traffic. Targeted devices would not need to be infected or controlled by the adversary; rather, hit-list generation techniques similar to those discussed in Chapter 5 could be used to locate hosts able to receive traffic. If this task can be repeated before the TBF timers expire, a denial of service attack becomes sustainable. In order to more explicitly characterize the bandwidth requirements, we model such an attack on Manhattan using well known parameters [131, 188]. Given an area of 31.1 miles^2 and a sector coverage area of approximately 0.5 and 0.75 miles^2, Manhattan contains 55 sectors. Using a READY timer of 5 seconds and 41 byte attack packets (i.e., TCP/IP headers plus one byte), the delivery of legitimate data services in Manhattan could be prevented with the attack shown below:

$$Capacity \approx 55 \text{ sectors} \times \frac{32 \text{ msgs}}{1 \text{ sector}} \times \frac{41 \text{ bytes}}{1 \text{ msg}} \times \frac{1}{5 \text{ sec}}$$
$$\approx 110 \; Kbps$$

The exhaustion of all hypothetical TBFs may not be necessary given current usage and deployed hardware. As the current demand for voice services far outpaces cellular data usage, only a small percentage of physical channels in a sector are used as PDCHs. Because GPRS/EDGE are not extremely high bandwidth services, allowing 32 individual flows to be concurrently multiplexed across a single PDCH would be detrimental to individual throughput. Accordingly, often only a subset of the 32 TBFs (4, 8 or 16 [116, 127]) are usable. The maximum number of concurrent TBFs in a sector is therefore $min(d * u, 32)$, where d is the number of downlink PDCHs and u is the maximum number of users per PDCH. While the number of PDCHs can be dynamically increased in response to rising demand for data services, networks typically hold unused channels to absorb spikes in voice calls. It is therefore unlikely that all 32 TBFs will be available at all times, if ever. A more realistic approximation of the bandwidth required to deny access to data services is given by:

$$Capacity \approx 55 \text{ sectors} \times \frac{4 \to 16 \text{ msgs}}{1 \text{ sector}} \times \frac{41 \text{ bytes}}{1 \text{ msg}} \times \frac{1}{5 \text{ sec}}$$
$$\approx 14.1 \to 56.4 \; Kbps$$

---

passed since the last exchange with the targeted device occurred, reaches its maximum value. Our description above is meant to simplify the exact mechanisms for the reader without loss of precision.

The brute-force method of attacking a cellular data network in a metropolitan setting is simply to saturate all of the physical channels with traffic. Even at their greatest levels of provisioning, the fastest cellular data services are simply no match against traffic generated by Internet-based adversaries [149, 168]. Such attacks, obvious by the sheer volume of traffic created, would likely be noticed and mitigated at the gateways to the network. However, with knowledge of the interaction between different network elements, it is possible for an adversary to launch a much smaller attack capable of achieving the same ends. A basic understanding of the packet delivery process provides the requisite information for realizing this attack.

Given a theoretical maximum capacity of 171.2 Kbps per frequency and as many as 8 allocated frequencies per sector, an adversary attempting the brute-force saturation of such a system would instead need to generate the volume of traffic as calculated as:

$$Capacity \approx 55 \text{ sectors} \times \frac{171.2 \text{ Kbps}}{1 \text{ frequency}} \times \frac{8 \text{ frequencies}}{1 \text{ sector}}$$
$$\approx 73.56 Mbps$$

By attacking the logical channels instead of the raw theoretical bandwidth, *an adversary can reduce the amount of traffic needed to deny service to a metropolitan area by as much as three orders of magnitude.* Note that networks implementing EDGE, which can provide three times the bandwidth of a GPRS system, would experience the same consequences given the same volume of attack traffic.

Simulation

To demonstrate the exploitation of delayed resource teardown, we simulate a GPRS network under varying traffic loads. Although the full complement of TBFs may not be available in all real deployments [116, 127], we conservatively allow for up to 32 concurrent flows. When in use, each TFI is held for exactly five seconds unless a new packet arrives. While it is possible for a single device to obtain multiple TFIs, we assume that all incoming flows for a given destination share a single TBF [14]. Finally, we observed that voice and data requests share control channels in real networks and therefore replace data control channels with their voice equivalents (i.e., RACH instead of PRACH) in our simulations.

Legitimate voice and data calls were modeled as Poisson random processes and generated at rates of 50,000 and 20,000 per hour, respectively, across Manhattan. The duration of these flows are also generated in a similar fashion with means of 120 and 10 seconds, respectively. These values represent standard volumes and exhibit no blocking. Attack flows, each consisting of a single packet, are also modeled by a Poisson random process with rates ranging from 100-200 Kbps. Each run, of which there were 1000 iterations for each

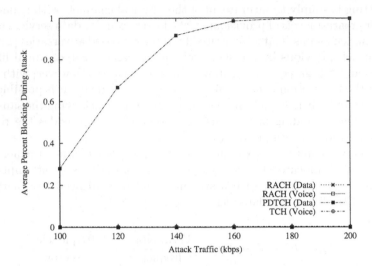

Fig. 6.5. Blocking of legitimate traffic for varying attack traffic loads. Note that blocking only occurs on the PDTCH. These loads represent the entire attack bandwidth used across Manhattan.

attack load, simulated an hour of time with attacks occupying the middle 30 minutes.

Figure 6.5 shows the blocking rates of legitimate traffic caused by an attack on the delayed teardown mechanism. At a rate of 160 Kbps or greater, the ability to use cellular data services within Manhattan is virtually nonexistent. The amount of traffic required to execute such an attack is slightly greater than the estimation of a perfect scenario in Section 6.4.2 due to the exponential interarrival rate used to generate packets. However, because this more realistically represents the nature of packet delivery in a network given the presence of other traffic, it offers a more accurate characterization of the attack. In spite of having the potential to deliver large volumes of traffic once flows are established, these results demonstrate that use of cellular data services can in fact be denied with less bandwidth than was used in the targeted text messaging attacks.

Figure 6.6 offers additional insight into the attack by providing the utilization profile for a number of channels. Most importantly, only the PDTCHs operate at capacity during the attack. This utilization represents the state of virtual resources, not channel bandwidth. None of the channels responsible for delivering voice, most critically the TCHs, are measurably affected by the increase in data traffic. Note that this is deliberate as cellular data services such as GPRS are designed to completely separate voice and data services.

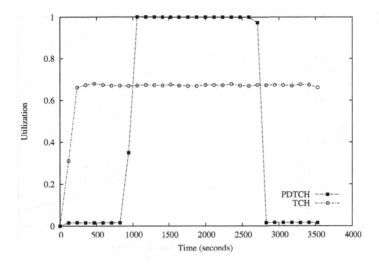

Fig. 6.6. TFI utilization for a Manhattan-wide attack at 200Kbps. Actual PDTCH utilization (not shown) is virtually zero because of infrequent arrivals for these established flows.

6.4.3 Exploiting Setup Mechanisms

Analysis

If connections to an end host must repeatedly be reestablished, the interarrival time between successive packets becomes exceedingly large. Delaying resource reclamation is therefore a necessary mechanism to ensure some semblance of continuous connectivity to the network. This latency, however, is not simply the result of the time required for a user to overhear an incoming paging request. To better understand setup cost, we examine a network in which resource reclamation occurs immediately after the last packet in a flow is received.

Of particular interest to such an analysis is the performance of the common uplink channel, the PRACH. Because this channel is shared by all hosts attempting to establish connections with the network, the PRACH inherently has the potential to be a system bottleneck. To minimize contention, access to the PRACH is mediated through the slotted-ALOHA protocol. Given a channel divided into timeslots of size t and time synchronization across hosts, end devices attempting to establish connections transmit requests at the beginning of a timeslot. In so doing, the network reduces the amount of time during which collision can occur from $2t$ in the random access case to t. While slotted-ALOHA offers a significant improvement over random access,

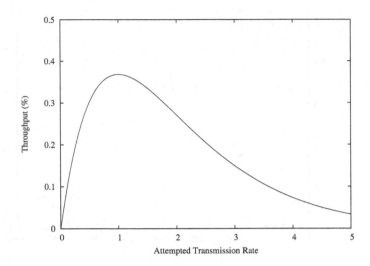

Fig. 6.7. The throughput profile of slotted-ALOHA. Note that the maximum throughput of a system implementing this algorithm is limited to 0.368.

its throughput remains low. Given a traffic intensity of G messages per unit time, the instantaneous probability of success (i.e., normalized throughput) γ of slotted-ALOHA is:

$$\gamma = Ge^{-G}$$

The maximum theoretical utilization of channel implementing slotted-ALOHA is 0.368, as shown in Figure 6.7. In reality, however, this value is significantly lower. As the number of incoming connection establishment requests increases, so too does the need for retransmission due to collision. Accordingly, the instantaneous nature of the above equation does not perfectly model feedback (i.e., retransmissions). Systems implementing slotted-ALOHA consequently slide far away from the equilibrium as traffic increases. Given a theoretically infinite number of retransmission retries, the throughput of such systems quickly approaches zero. The throughput of real systems therefore typically stabilizes at a point far below this optimum value. Accordingly, this channel can easily be made into a bottleneck.

Given a large number of paging requests, potentially caused by the immediate reclamation of resources as described above, the throughput of this already constrained channel would be severely degraded. Accordingly, the rate at which responses to connection establishment requests will pass through this channel is much lower than the available bandwidth. Because of the significant

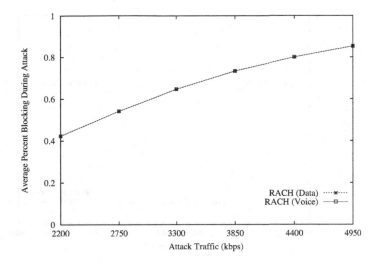

Fig. 6.8. Blocking caused when immediate resource reclamation is enforced on data sessions. Notice that because both voice and data flows use the RACH, increased data requests cause voice blocking. No blocking was observed on other channels.

number of customizable variables, we leave the discussion of specific settings to the simulations below.

Simulation

To characterize the impact of frequent connection reestablishment on a cellular data network, we simulate a variety of traffic levels in the presence of immediate resource recovery. Specifically, when the base station no longer has packets to send for a particular flow, the targeted device returns to the STANDBY state. Except for delayed teardown procedures, all network settings and conditions including legitimate traffic volumes and interarrival patterns, remain the same. Attacks in this scenario, each of which occurs according to a Poisson random distribution, range from 2200-4950 Kbps spread across all of Manhattan. As in our previous experiments, each attack traffic level was run for 1000 iterations.

Figure 6.8 shows the blocking rates for legitimate traffic on a number of channels. Unlike the attack in the previous section, in which PDTCH blocking occurred because of TBF exhaustion, no loss of packets was observed on the PDTCHs. In spite of this, the results of these simulations confirm a more significant vulnerability - both voice and data flows experience blocking on the RACH. Although such networks strive to separate voice and data traffic,

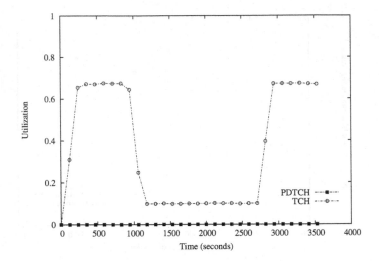

Fig. 6.9. The impact of RACH congestion on voice calls. Notice that during the attack phase, voice call blocking on the RACH causes a significant under utilization of traffic channels.

the dual use of control channels allows misbehavior in one realm to affect the other. Generating just over 3 Mbps of traffic for the entire city of Manhattan, an adversary is capable of blocking nearly 65% of all traffic - voice and data. For a network in which a blocking probability of 1% is typically viewed as unacceptable, such an attack represents a serious operational crisis.

Figure 6.9 provides further information about the impact of the 4950Kbps attack on voice and data services. The most notable consequence of this attack is observable in the nearly 80% decrease in TCH utilization. The near zero utilization of PDTCHs offers an explanation to the lack of blocking observed in the previous figure - the majority of legitimate traffic is being filtered out before it can ever be delivered by the PDTCHs. Accordingly, a network using the settings described above is subject to attacks capable of denying both voice and data services.

6.5 Conflicts in Network Design

At first glance, the differences between each of the attacks on cellular networks appear stark. Targeted text messaging attacks fill and maintain a low-bandwidth control channel at capacity. Adversaries attacking cellular data services exhaust virtual resources or take advantage of access protocol inefficiencies. In reality, all of these vulnerabilities are remnants of a conflict

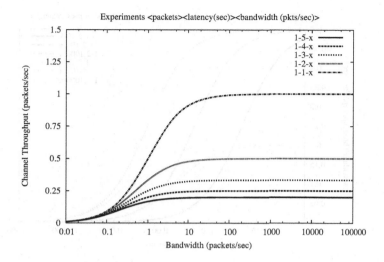

Fig. 6.10. Given a connection establishment latency and the size of requests (in packets), we examine the impact of varying bandwidth on system throughput. When the available bandwidth allows for the virtually instantaneous delivery of requests, system throughput plateaus. This result indicates that bandwidth is ultimately not the bottleneck in this system. (log-scale)

between the design philosophies of telecommunications and traditional data networks. Specifically, they are the result of contrasting definitions of a flow and the role of networks in establishing them. To make such a claim more concrete, we begin by demonstrating how a pair of seemingly adequate techniques for mitigating the above attacks fails to do so.

The most obvious approach to addressing these data attacks is to expand the range of possible TFI values. Unfortunately, as mentioned earlier, these limitations are necessary given the bandwidth available to GRPS/EDGE networks. The use of 32 (or fewer) concurrent flows per sector is a requisite concession for providing basic levels of connectivity between the network and end devices. In order for an increased pool of identifiers to have a meaningful effect, the bandwidth available to data services would also need to be significantly increased. This combination of approaches is actually implemented in 3G cellular networks such as UMTS [23]. However, even these networks suffer from the high cost of connection establishment (i.e., delivering the first packet in a flow).

A session establishment period lasting a few seconds represents only a small fraction of the total lifetime for a connection persisting for a number of minutes. Given the limited amount of spectrum allocated to cellular providers,

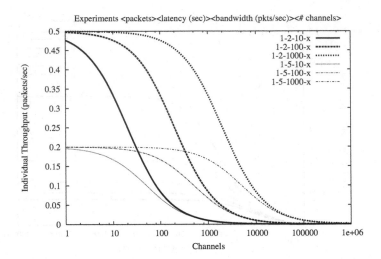

Fig. 6.11. Increasing the number of channels can improve overall system through-put. However, individual throughputs and connection setup times react inversely. Reducing the expense of connection establishment must therefore come from a reduction in connection setup latency. (log-scale)

such infrequently used channels predictably occupy as little space as possible to avoid wasting bandwidth. Because the duration of a packet flow may not provide sufficient time over which such an expense can be amortized, the minimal allocation of bandwidth to connection establishment may in fact create a system bottleneck. To capture the impact of additional bandwidth on connection setup, we offer a simple model of request throughput for a sector as follows:

$$Throughput = \frac{\# \; Packets}{Setup \; Latency + \frac{\# \; Packets}{Bandwidth}}$$

If the expense associated with connection establishment was the result of inadequate resources, an increase in bandwidth should alleviate much of this cost. Such a scenario would be equivalent to increasing the size of the smallest link in a traditional data network to improve end-to-end throughput. However, the calculated effects of increased bandwidth on overall throughput are extremely limited in this setting. Because connection establishment exchanges contain fixed-length messages and not the variably sized packets of data delivery, the presence of additional bandwidth does little to improve performance after each channel can send paging requests instantaneously. As is shown in Figure 6.10, the limit of system throughput as bandwidth approaches infinity becomes:

$$\lim_{BW \to \infty} Throughput = \frac{\# \ Packets}{Setup \ Latency}$$

Increasing system throughput can, for this reason, be accomplished in one of two ways. In the first, the number of channels over which connections can be sent could be increased. Such a change would allow many more connection establishment requests to be sent in parallel. While increasing the throughput of the system as a whole, this approach would prove detrimental to individual users. As shown in Figure 6.11, subdividing a fixed bandwidth into additional channels intuitively reduces the throughput of a single user. Adding extra channels could also potentially create elevated contention for the shared uplink channel (RACH). More importantly, increasing the throughput of the system does not necessarily reduce cost with respect to delay experienced by individual users. Therefore,

> Decreasing the cost of connection establishment in a cellular data network is not a matter of increasing bandwidth but rather the reduction of connection setup latency.

The concept of connection establishment is considerably different in cellular and traditional data networks. In the case of the former, the network must page, wake, and negotiate with a targeted device before ultimately delivering traffic. Whether due to misaligned sleep cycles, missed paging messages or congestion, this set of operations can require several seconds before being able to transmit data. As discussed in Section 6.4, these concessions are made because the network assumes that end devices are limited both in terms of power and computational ability. True packet-switched networks provide no such services; rather, higher layers in the protocol stack implement functionality as needed. In general, each packet is treated as an individual entity and is simply forwarded to the next logical hop. Whether it is wired or wireless in nature, there is no connection to be established from the perspective of the network[4]. Nodes responsible for routing packets do not assume that their next hop neighbors have any specific abilities other than moving the packet closer to its intended destination. Accordingly, connection setup latency is more accurately depicted as propagation delay from the viewpoint of these networks. Given that the delay of propagation time and connection establishment differ by many orders of magnitude, the underlying cause of low-bandwidth attacks on cellular data networks becomes more clear.

The vulnerable components in both the targeted text messaging and cellular data service attacks are those mechanisms responsible for translating

---

[4] We consider connection establishment in terms of individual flows. Initial access to almost every network has a cost (authentication, etc). This startup cost, however, is amortized in both settings.

traffic from one network architecture to another. While a data network simply forwards individual packets as they arrive, a cellular data network interprets the first packet in a flow as an indicator of more traffic to come. Rather than simply forward that packet to its final destination, the network dedicates significant processing and bandwidth resources to ensure that the end device is ready to receive data. This assumption is valid in traditional telephony because of the nature of voice communication. Except for cases of an immediate hangup, sessions are guaranteed to contain multiple "packets" of information. Data communications, however, do not necessarily share this characteristic. Any protocol or application generating packets separated by a number of seconds (e.g., instant messaging programs, session keep-alive messages, applications implementing Nagle's algorithm [128]) violates this model. Whether it is embodied by text messages or data traffic, the amplification of a single incoming packet into a series of expensive delay inducing setup operations is the source of such attacks. Figure 6.12 reinforces this conclusion by comparing generalizations of the two architectures.

Connection establishment in cellular and traditional networks are so different because the philosophies upon which these systems are based are incompatible. The notion that the middle of a network provide only a limited set of simple functions is at the core of the end-to-end principle [158]. By making no assumptions about the context in which a packet's contents will be used, the network is free to specialize in a single task - moving data. Services not used by all applications, including reliable delivery, content confidentiality and in-order arrival, become the responsibility of higher layers of the protocol stack in the end hosts. The concentration on sending packets allows networks built according to the end-to-end principle to be flexible enough to support new application types and usage models as they emerge. Telecommunications networks are built on the opposite model. Hard service requirements, especially for real-time interaction, and attempts to optimize for battery constraints forced the network to provide the majority of service guarantees. Because the functionality of the network was once limited to voice applications, telecommunications systems could be tightly tailored to a specific set of constraints. The inclination to build a network in such a manner was addressed by the original end-to-end argument:

> "Because the communications subsystem is frequently specified before the applications that use the subsystem are known, the designer may be tempted to "help" the users by taking on more function than necessary." [158]

Because these specialized networks implement more functionality than is absolutely necessary, they exhibit *rigidity*, or the inability to adapt to meet changing requirements or usage [52]. Rigidity in design causes such systems to enforce assumptions appropriate for one subset of traffic on all others. The treatment of each packet as part of a larger flow is one embodiment of such inflexibility. This rigidity is also apparent when examined from the

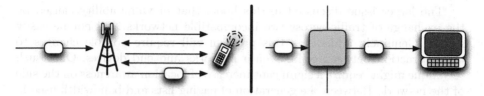

Fig. 6.12. A comparison of the cost of delivering a single packet in cellular and traditional data networks. In the cellular data case (left), a significant amount of delay is added because of connection establishment procedures, whereas the router in the traditional setting (right) simply forwards the packet to the final hop.

perspective of evolving end devices. For example, many laptops now contain hardware supplying access to cellular data networks [145, 85]. Regardless of their ability to implement services at higher layers of the protocol stack or their access to power, these end devices are forced to transition between STANDBY and READY states simply because such behavior is mandated by the network. Devices connecting via 802.11 could simply trade off the overhead associated with paging at the cost of additional power use. This point is made more obvious when put in the context of home or office LANs supported by a cellular backhaul connection. The network would require such systems to participate in the process of location determination and connection establishment in spite of their lack of mobility. By building assumptions and services into the network itself, the system as a whole is made less flexible. When conditions change and assumptions fail to hold, the rigidity of cellular data systems causes them to break.

6.6 Efficient Mitigation of Data Network Vulnerabilities

Addressing the specific attacks detailed in this and the previous chapter may be realistic in the short term. Optimized paging techniques [112, 27] may help to reduce search time and its resulting delay. As was done with the SMS attacks in Chapter 5, techniques from queue and resource management could be used to mitigate blocking on the RACH. The move to 3G and a significantly larger pool of identifiers would reduce the practical likelihood of virtual resource exhaustion. While such methods would indeed mitigate many of the example vulnerabilities discussed in this work, a strategy for building robust cellular data systems based on constant patching would ultimately fail. All of the above solutions merely treat the symptoms of a larger problem. Accordingly, as long as there is a disconnect between the ways in which data is delivered in cellular and traditional data systems, exploitable mechanisms will exist. Such mechanisms need not be limited to the wireless portion of the network; rather, any component of the core network involved in establishing a session will be vulnerable.

The larger issue discussed in this book, that of vulnerability caused by the exchange of traffic across two incompatible networks, will not be easily solved. Genuinely addressing this problem will require notable changes to the interaction between cellular data networks and end devices. Once such technique might require a significant increase of location awareness on the side of the network. Between the generation of paging lists and bandwidth used in multiple sectors, significant processing resources and time are spent finding a device each time a connection establishment occurs. Instead of knowing that a device is serviced by a potentially large set of base stations, an improved system might require location update information from a device each time it moves between sectors. Used in concert with much shorter sleep cycles, such an improvement to location knowledge may make the elimination of paging possible. This approach, however, would have a serious impact on resources in both end devices and the network. From the user perspective, increased monitoring and interaction with the network would negatively impact battery life. In the case of the latter, the overhead needed to process such an increase in messaging would also affect network performance. A more radical approach would be to replace cellular data services with a new high-bandwidth wireless protocol. Instead of necessarily sharing bandwidth and timeslotting schemes with voice communications, this new protocol would be assigned to a separate portion of the spectrum. In so doing, designers of the new data system would not be constrained by any of the rigidity forced upon current cellular data networks. In addition to technical tradeoffs, this solution would also need to deal with the complexities involved in spectrum allocation - reducing its viability for the foreseeable future.

These comments should not be seen as an endorsement of any technology or architecture over another. Instead, they are simply the product of an observation of the impact on availability caused by interconnecting diametrically opposed methods of system design. Being beholden to a specific architecture and failing to understand the problems caused by linking such networks are in fact the causes of the rigidity seen in this system. It is highly unlikely that similar thinking will correct the problem.

6.7 Summary

In this chapter, we have presented a number of vulnerabilities in General Packet Radio Service (GPRS) and Enhanced Data rates for GSM Evolution (EDGE) systems. Under normal operating conditions, these services provide high speed data service to cellular subscribers without requiring individual devices to monopolize the air interface. Unfortunately, expensive setup and teardown mechanisms allow an adversary to deny service to high speed cellular data services in metropolitan areas using less bandwidth than was required to attack the low bandwidth SMS system. Using only 160kbps of traffic, such attacks have the potential to block more than 96% of data traffic requests.

Because of combined control channels, voice services can also be affected by such attacks.

In spite of providing packet-switched services on the air interface, these attacks demonstrate that cellular networks remain circuit-switched systems. Because the network takes on responsibilities not generally associated with traditional IP networks (e.g., waking a machine from sleep mode), cellular networks are susceptible to attack. This vulnerability highlights the complications caused when networks built on the End-to-End principle with those that are customized to specific kinds of traffic. Accordingly, cellular networks will be vulnerable to attack at all places where traffic is translated between the two architectures.

Addressing such vulnerabilities is therefore a systemic issue. While patches addressing the specific attacks detailed in this work can help to alleviate such attacks, such mechanisms are likely to exacerbate vulnerabilities elsewhere in the system. Significant open security challenges therefore face the telecommunications infrastructure as it evolves to support a wider variety of traffic types.

Vulnerabilities in Voice over IP

The fundamental nature of telecommunications has changed rapidly in our lifetimes. At their advent, such systems were designed to allow people to call locations with the hope of locating a specific recipient on the other end. As technology evolved to allow individuals increased freedom of movement, such a static phone system failed to provide the connectivity needed to support communication in a mobile society. As a reflection, cellular networks emerged as a means of connecting callers to a device typically carried by the intended recipient. However, such systems still fail to connect a caller to a specific recipient when the targeted device fails or is unavailable. In spite of such significant advances, these systems fundamentally do not connect a person to another person.

The emergence of *Voice over IP* (VoIP) provides such an opportunity. VoIP uses traditional data communication networks such as the Internet to deliver packetized voice between a sender and receiver. More critically, many of the protocol suites instantiating VoIP allow for the direct connection of calling and receiving parties by seamlessly routing calls to the device currently used by the receiver. Moreover, by doing so using packet-switched networks, these systems gain a significant throughput improvement over traditional telecommunications networks.

With this fundamental shift and its benefits therefore come significant security and reliability issues. The mixing of traffic with real-time constraints with other data streams, the presence of a wider array of adversaries and a far more open network infrastructure should all create an increased security focus on these systems. However, VoIP protocols and architectures are only beginning to be analyzed by the security community.

In this chapter, we present an overview of VoIP and the protocols and architectures supporting it in both next generation telecommunications networks and the larger Internet. We begin by examining how such protocols and architectures have evolved from a historical perspective. We then explore the *Session Initiation Protocol* (SIP), its current security mechanisms and their shortcomings in depth. Our examination then evaluates a number of open problems being explored by the research community. Finally, we finish with a brief discussion of how such systems can be securely constructed. By understanding how such systems operate and why they are currently vulnerable, the community at large can begin to address the fundamental problems facing telecommunications systems built on a foundation of VoIP.

7.1 History and Description

Access to the hardware and software necessary to run an SS7 network has always been somewhat limited. Accordingly, use of this set of standards outside of telecommunications providers is rare. As general-purpose computing hardware became more readily available and the Internet Protocol (IP) became more widespread, new building blocks for a telecommunications infrastructure arose. However, unlike their predecessors, these new networks were built upon a foundation of packet-switched networks. Accordingly, none of the real-time guarantees associated with circuit-switched systems were immediately inherited by these new systems. Experimentation with this new infrastructure led to the creation of initial standards for transmitting multimedia data including H.261 [89] and H.320 [91] as early as the mid 1980's. These early attempts demonstrated not only the possibility for packet-switched multimedia, but also the need for more advanced IP telephony standards.

The first standard to address telephony in IP networks was H.323. First approved by the *International Telecommunication Union* (ITU) in 1996, H.323 is a comprehensive voice and video telephony system built from the perspective of the telecommunications industry [92]. Call models similar to those in traditional landline telephone networks simplify the exchange of calls between H.323 IP networks and the PSTN. From widespread consumer product offerings (e.g., Microsoft NetMeeting, Cisco and Avaya IP Phones) to PSTN providers running H.323 in portions of their networks, the combination of being "first to the market" and ease of interoperability with the available telecommunications infrastructure helped to quickly ensure the success of this standard.

Another standard for VoIP has received much greater attention in recent years. Around the same time as the first approved draft of H.323 appeared, the *Multiparty Multimedia Session Control* (MMUSIC) workgroup within the *Internet Engineering Task Force* (IETF) began developing SIP [95]. Formally becoming an IETF standard in 1999, SIP is built from the perspective of the Internet community. As we will discuss later in this chapter, SIP therefore relies more heavily on the currently deployed infrastructure of data networks (e.g., DNS). Much like H.323, a wide variety of products and services supporting and using SIP are also available (e.g., Vonage VoIP service, Cisco and Avaya IP Phones).

It is unclear whether H.323 or SIP will prevail as the sole VoIP standard. Issues of interoperability and supported features are continuously being addressed by both communities. As a reflection of this, a large portion of currently available VoIP phones in fact support both standards and allow users to configure their systems as needed. However, because the network core of next generation cellular networks will be based on SIP, the remainder of this chapter will focus on this standard.

7.2 Session Initiation Protocol

SIP is a session establishment framework. Instead of simply connecting parties, SIP allows parties to negotiate the terms of their call. Accordingly, sessions requiring audio, video, encryption or any other service allow each terminal to set preferred codecs and algorithms. Those parties not using a feature are simply not obliged to support it. Accordingly, a wide range of devices, from high-end multiparty video conferencing systems to simple office phones, can interact through SIP.

Before discussing its role in the next generation core network, known as the *IP Multimedia Subsystem* (IMS), we present a basic overview of SIP. This is by no means an exhaustive examination of the topic; rather, we seek to provide readers with a working knowledge of the subject. Those interested in learning more about SIP should consult any number of additional resources [157, 154, 137, 167, 60].

7.2.1 Architecture

When compared to a cellular network, the number of nodes specifically dedicate to supporting SIP is significantly reduced. Such a simplification is largely the result of the reuse of the available data networks infrastructure. Because SIP operates at the application layer, the majority of duties, from routing to reliability, are addressed by the lower layers of the protocol stack. However, functions including the location of specific devices and the negotiation of session parameters must be handled by application layer processes.

The most critical component of a SIP network is the *SIP registrar*. In order to support not only the mobility of a user across domains, but also of a user across devices, the SIP registrar is responsible for tracking the current device and its corresponding domain. The registrar allows a user to subscribe to receive certain services including network information updates, voice mailbox state changes and instant messaging "buddy lists" [154]. Accordingly, the SIP registrar is in many ways analogous to a user's HLR in a GSM network and, like HLRs, are therefore typically managed on a per-domain/autonomous system basis.

Users wishing to initiate calls using SIP typically rely on a *SIP proxy*. SIP proxies typically mask the complexities associated with locating a remote user. For instance, when a call request is initiated from Alice to Bob in Figure 7.1, Alice's request is initially sent to the address associated with Bob's registrar.

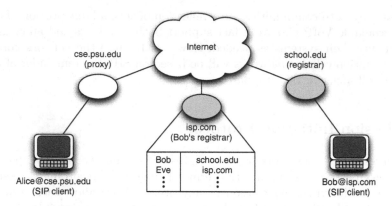

Fig. 7.1. A high level overview of the SIP architecture.

In this case, the proxy attempts to contact Bob in the `isp.com` domain. The registrar responds to the proxy with a message indicating that Bob is currently located in the `school.edu` domain. The proxy can then forward the call request to Bob in his current location without forcing the user's SIP client to transmit multiple requests.

The presence of SIP registrars and proxies is not required as specified above. If two parties always communicate between static IP addresses, neither proxies nor registrars are necessary. As the number of users in a system and the mobility of those users increases, however, managing calls without the assistance of these devices quickly becomes cumbersome. The separation of proxy from registrar is also not a requirement in real systems. Such processes are often only logically separated and run on the same server. Separation of the proxy and registration services may only become necessary as the volume of traffic approaches carrier levels. The mix of processes dedicated to handling SIP traffic is therefore a deployment specific issue, and should be treated on a case by case basis.

7.2.2 SIP Messages

Encoding

The constraints of traditional telephony systems placed rigid constraints on the encoding of signaling. As discussed in Chapter 3, even modern cellular systems dedicate only small portions of their total bandwidth to the delivery of control data. Accordingly, the compactness of such information is typically valued over human readability and ease of implementation. The use of standards such as ASN.1 in current cellular and H.323 networks is a direct reflection of this reality.

SIP approaches the problem of encoding from the opposite perspective. Given that the average bandwidth available to a device connected to the In-

Table 7.1. SIP Commands

Command	Function
ACK	An acknowledgment of a previous message.
BYE	Indicates that the other party has disconnected/hung up.
CANCEL	Cancels a previous request made by a client.
INFO	Used to communicate control information during a call.
INVITE	Indicates a session request between the sender and receiver.
MESSAGE	Carries instant messaging (IM) content.
NOTIFY	Sent to notify the receiver of a change in a resource or call state.
OPTIONS	Returns the capabilities of the receiver.
PRACK	Acknowledges a provisional response.
PUBLISH	Publishes event state.
REFER	Indicates the address of a third-party a recipient should contact.
REGISTER	Alerts a SIP Proxy of the current location of a user.
SUBSCRIBE	Registers a client for NOTIFY messages updating the change of some resource.
UPDATE	Allows a client to change session settings (e.g., codec)

ternet is significantly higher than one connected to a cellular network, the need for compact data encoding is less necessary. This, coupled with the more open nature of development in the Internet community, led the designers of SIP to opt for simplicity over efficiency. As a reflection of this philosophy, SIP messages are carried as ASCII-encoded HTTP requests. Messages are therefore easily parsed and interpreted by widely available software. The overhead of signaling, however, can grow quickly and require multiple packets to be transmitted to deliver individual commands between hosts.

Addressing

Unlike traditional phone numbers, which represent the area code, exchange code and terminal number[1], users identified by an email-like SIP identity called a *Uniform Resource Identifier* (URI). For instance, calls to the user Alice in Figure 7.1 would be addressed to `sip:alice@cse.psu.edu`. Because the SIP registrar allows calls destined for Alice to be forwarded, calls sent to this URI can be delivered to any device in any domain supporting SIP.

Message Types

SIP implements a number of simple message types in order to support IP telephony. These messages allow clients to establish, maintain and tear down voice, video and data sessions for point-to-point and point-to-multipoint communications. Table 7.1 offers a comprehensive list and brief descriptions of these message types. We highlight the most commonly used types below.

---

[1] See Chapter 5 for a discussion of the NPA-NXX-XXXX structure.

Much like when cellular phones are powered on, SIP devices and software must alert the network of their readiness to receive calls. Accordingly, a SIP client transmits a *REGISTER* message to its SIP registrar in order to inform the network of its contact information (i.e., current IP address). When a client is not registered with its domain registrar, incoming calls are either refused or deferred to a mailbox (either voicemail or a text response). In order to establish a session with another party, a SIP client sends an *INVITE* message to its proxy, which locates the targeted individual. An example of an INVITE request from Alice to Bob from Figure 7.1 is shown below:

```
INVITE sip:bob@isp.com SIP/2.0
VIA: SIP/2.0/UDP 130.203.4.2
Max-Forwards: 70
From: sip:alice@university.edu
To: sip:bob@isp.com
Call-ID: 450a533d@isp.com
Content-Type: application/sdp
Content-Length: 101

v=0
c=IN IP4 130.203.4.2
m=audio 37777 RTP/AVP 0
```

As previously mentioned, the INVITE request is encoded as an ASCII message. Like all HTTP requests, the first line of the request indicates the message type (INVITE), address (`sip:bob@isp.com`), protocol (SIP) and version (2.0) of the included message. The second line, VIA, specifies the transport protocol (TCP or UDP) used to deliver the message and the path taken by the message thus far. Max-Forwards limits the number of proxies a message can transit through, and is generally set to a default value of 70 hops. This field is largely used to detect routing loops. As expected, the "To:" and "From:" fields indicate the source and destination parties involved in the session. Call-ID is used to uniquely identify each session, as multiple session may occur concurrently. The remaining portion of the message contains the negotiable aspects of the session, encoded using the *Session Description Protocol [31]*. Here, the sender is using SDP version 0, requesting that responses be sent to 130.203.4.2 and asking that audio be sent to port 37777 using the *Realtime Transport Protocol* (RTP) and encoded in AVP 0 (PCM μ-law, as described in Chapter 3).

Additional messages are used to support SIP telephony sessions. If both parties agree to start a session, the sender transmits an *ACK* to the receiver before beginning the call itself. If no agreement can be reached (e.g., no compatible codecs are available), either party can respond with a *CANCEL* message. Calls are then ended by transmitting a *BYE* message.

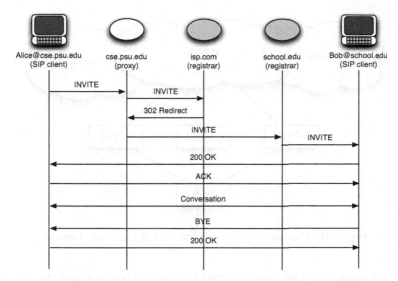

Fig. 7.2. A sample SIP call. Because Bob is not in his home domain, the registrar in the `isp.com` domain tells Alice's proxy his current location. In order to allow for negotiation, the INVITE and 200 OK response both contain the codecs preferred by Alice and Bob, respectively. After the call is connected and their business completed, Bob terminates the call by sending the BYE command and receives a 200 OK from Alice's machine as confirmation.

7.2.3 Making Phone Calls

Using the previous presented information as a basis, we now present a high-level overview of a SIP call. Figure 7.2 offers a graphical representation of the operations.

When Alice wishes to make a SIP call to Bob, her SIP client transmits an INVITE message to her SIP proxy. The proxy converts Bob's URI into an IP address using DNS and then forwards the request to the corresponding SIP registrar. Because Bob is currently at school and not at this home, the SIP registrar returns an HTTP redirect message (302 Found) to Alice's proxy. Alice's proxy takes the redirection address and forwards her request to the registrar in Bob's current domain, `school.com`. Bob's SIP client receives the message and agrees to use the codecs specified in the INVITE message. In his HTTP response (200 OK), Bob can request a different set of codecs for the channel delivered to Alice. If Alice can support Bob's request, she replies with a SIP ACK message and the session begins. Throughout the course of the call, multimedia packets are delivered using RTP. The delivery of these packets is controlled using the *RTP Control Protocol* (RTCP).

When the conversation reaches its conclusion, each participant must "hang up". Here, Bob ends the call first and therefore sends a SIP BYE message to the Alice. To indicate her reception of the end of the conversation, Alice's

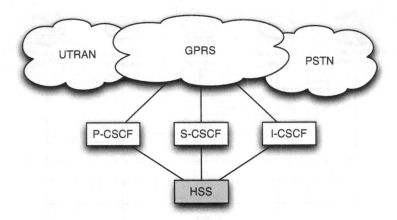

Fig. 7.3. The network architecture of IMS cellular systems.

SIP client returns an OK message (200 OK) to Bob's client and the session is terminated.

Note that calls can occur in a peer-to-peer fashion (directly between Alice and Bob) or through their respective proxies if billing is a requirement of the network. Alternatively, signaling can occur through the centralized infrastructure and voice traffic can operate in a peer to peer fashion. This is in direct contrast to SS7-based cellular networks, in which signaling information and voice traffic must traverse through the same nodes.

7.3 IP-Multimedia Subsystem Network

7.3.1 IMS Architecture

The next generation of wireless cellular networks will migrate to use Internet technologies. These systems will be called the *IP Multimedia Subsystem* (IMS). To establish calls and manage services, SIP is used. As such, devices are addressed by a *Uniform Resource Identifier* (URI).

Several new network elements are introduced that acts as SIP proxies and registrars. A high level architecture of IMS is shown in Figure 7.3. The HLR is replaced with a *Home Subscriber Server* (HSS), and the MSCs and VLRs are replaced with *Call Server Control Functions* (CSCFs). These servers may play the role of a gateway MSC via a combination of an *Interrogator CSCF* (I-CSCF) and *Serving CSCF* (S-CSCF), or serving MSC (Proxy CSCF - P-CSCF).

When a user registers with the network, it typically is assigned a P-CSCF to which it directly exchanges its signaling messages. All communication with the home network is done through the I-CSCF. The role of the I-CSCF is to hide the deployment details of the IMS core network from the access networks.

A S-CSCF is assigned to the user based on the capabilities of the user device and the types of services it will receive. This information is stored in an HSS that is assigned to a user based on its URI.

When a call is placed to a user, the SIP messages are routed to its home network on the basis of the domain of the URI. This message will be received by an I-CSCF which will query the HSS to locate the S-CSCF of the called user. The SIP messages are redirected to the S-CSCF which interacts with the P-CSCF to execute the signaling procedures.

Unlike the current mobile network, in IMS the SIP messages only locate devices and negotiate session parameters. They do not reserve network resources. Thus user information exchanged during a call will be routed independently of the path taken by the SIP messages.

SIP may also be used to provide other services, such as messaging.

7.3.2 Making Phone Calls

There are many possible network configurations for IMS which affect the details of how sessions are established. Here we present a simplified flow. As with regular SIP calls discussed above, the call is originated by an INVITE generated by a calling party. Here we concentrate on the message flow within the IMS network, i.e., after the INVITE message arrives at the border of the wireless service provider using IMS.

Before receiving any session requests, an IMS user must register with the network. When this occurs, the HSS is notified and assigns the user a S-CSCF based on the user (or devices) capabilities. When an INVITE message arrives at the IMS network it is received by an I-CSCF. Different requests will be handled by different I-CSCFs, so these entities do not maintain state for registered users. Instead they query the HSS to determine the S-CSCF assigned to the user.

When this information is returned to the I-CSCF, it sends an INVITE message to the S-CSCF assigned to the user. This S-CSCF invokes any service logic required for the session. Once this is complete, the S-CSCF forwards the INVITE either directly to a P-CSCF if the user is in its home network, or to the terminating network if the user is roaming.

These initial invite messages carry the SDP Offer that describes the desired session. At this point, the end-points exchange a series of Offer Responses and Confirmations to agree upon the session parameters. These are received and processed by the all CSCFs involved in establishing the session. Once the user accepts the incoming session request, it generates a 200 OK back to the originator.

7.4 IMS Versus Pure Internet Telephony

SIP was defined to enable many possible deployments. These ranged from pure peer-to-peer session establishment, to more sophisticated arrangements that leverage network-based proxies and registrars. This flexibility drives the attractiveness of SIP. Individual users may install SIP to communicate directly without the need to engage telephony service providers; these users may install or implement their own services. Alternatively, corporations or service providers may deploy proxies and registrars to implement services required for applications like call centers, call forking, or find-me services.

IMS defines a set of network instantiations that use SIP. The IMS standards were written from the perspective of wireless service providers. The architecture and protocol usage allows for network-based services and billing. Even these standards, however, do not dictate a specific deployment. Instead they define functions that together allow a service provider to build a network and operate it in an environment in which multiple service providers may be involved in a single session. Concerns include allowing for manageability of a service provider's network, supporting cross-network signaling and interoperability with existing wireless telecommunication standards such as GSM.

With this motivation, one can see the rationale for many of the defined functions in IMS. I-CSCFs are gateways into networks; they hide the internals of a network from other service providers. HSSs store profiles and location information so that subscribers may have seamless access to their services, much in the same way that they do in current wireless cellular networks. After all, most subscribers are not cognizant, nor do they care, which technology is being used to deliver their service as long as it works! CSCFs are assigned by the HSS depending on the capabilities and services subscribed to by the subscriber so that network-based services may be delivered.

With IMS, service providers can use SIP to provide enhanced services in an Internet environment while maintaining control for administrative purposes such as management and billing. Subscribers that do not wish to concern themselves with installing services on their end devices receive network-based services. Of course, these subscribers may always choose to use SIP to signal directly to another endpoint to establish communication using the wireless data portion of the emerging cellular networks and thus achieve peer-to-peer SIP control if they desire.

7.5 Wireless Issues

Providing voice services over broadband packet-switched networks is becoming commonplace. Companies including Skype[2] [166] and Vonage [190] provide free and/or low-cost VoIP to subscribers with a high speed connection to the Internet. In spite of their success in wired networks, attempts to port such applications to cellular networks have largely been met with failure. While popular opinion tends to blame cellular providers for policies preventing the

---

[2] Skype uses neither H.323 nor SIP. Instead, Skype relies upon its own proprietary protocol to provide VoIP services.

use of such applications, the implementation of packet-switched telephony in current cellular data networks faces a significant number of technological challenges.

Bandwidth constraints represent one of the major hurdles in realizing cellular VoIP service. As discussed in Chapter 6, networks implementing GRPS and EDGE can provide theoretical throughputs of up to 21.4 and 59.2kbps per channel, respectively. In reality, however, users experience performance well below these levels. Wireless interference, for instance, typically requires the use of robust coding schemes that incorporate error correction (i.e., throughput at the above speeds is only possible with coding schemes containing no error correction). While the specific coding scheme will vary, local conditions may require a degradation of throughput to theoretical maximums of 9.05 and 8.8kbps [21] for GPRS and EDGE, respectively. Even when using coding schemes with high levels of error correction, factors ranging from signal occluding landscape features (e.g., buildings) to improperly shielded electronic equipment cause some portion of packets to simply be lost in transmission. Accordingly, while the network may be capable of sending traffic at relatively high rates, consistent reception of packets by the client at such high speeds is extremely difficult. With common voice codecs such as PCM μ-law (see Chapter 3) requiring a stable bandwidth of 13kbps, current systems are unlikely to be able to dependably support high quality VoIP traffic.

Behaviors specific to cellular data networks may also greatly impact the quality of VoIP service. As discussed in Chapter 6, when a device in the READY state does not receive packets for a few seconds, it transitions to the power-saving STANDBY state. Upon the arrival of new packets, the network must re-page and prepare the intended destination device to receive traffic. Brief silence in a conversation (also called clipping) is therefore likely to cause extended periods of quiet due to the temporal expense associate with re-establishing a connection between the network and end device [185]. The queuing behavior implemented by the base station may also cause significant problems. Other types of cellular data networks, such as *Evolution - Data Optimized* (EV-DO) systems, deliver packets to wireless users in large bursts. When the base station scheduler selects a user, it attempts to transmit all packets queued for that user. The user in question is then unlikely to be serviced again until the majority of other users have received packets. [3] While such a strategy is appropriate for web browsing (in which all content can typically be delivered in one burst), users experience significant choppiness due to the irregular delivery of voice traffic.

In spite of these challenges, the talk of VoIP to mobile devices is increasing. However, most of these efforts have been focused on hybrid cellular/802.11 devices. While future evolutions of cellular data networks may better support VoIP natively (e.g., WiMAX [195], *Enhanced Version - Data and Voice* (EVDV)), current cellular-only data systems will struggle to sup-

---

[3] Dependent upon the exact scheduling algorithm used by the network.

port packet-based telephony. The deployment of such systems in selected markets [146, 194] is now beginning; however, it is unclear when widespread coverage will be available.

7.6 Security Issues

Given the range of telecommunications technology we have examined in this book, a natural question arises: "Which is the most secure?" The debate is, to say the least, heated. The isolation from other systems traditionally enjoyed by telecommunications networks has lead many to declare that our current infrastructure is more secure than emerging VoIP solutions. Other experts point to the potential to use a variety of cryptographic protocols in conjunction with SIP as the reason that evolving standards offer better security. We attempt to inform the above question as a resounding "it depends." As with all topics in security, it is necessary to define a threat model before attempting to address a problem.

Eavesdropping is typically the metric of choice when comparing VoIP to the circuit-switched infrastructure. In the PSTN and early cellular networks, monitoring the calls of a target was more often than not a matter of knowing where to listen. In the case of the former (and as seen in far too many detective movies), the use of a ladder, alligator clips and a phone attached to old analog landlines was once enough to accomplish such a task.[4] Less sophisticated tools, including walkie-talkies, can also intercept calls if a target uses a cordless phone. In cellular systems such as AMPS, a receiver tuned to the correct frequency could achieve the same result if they were within a reasonable proximity of a subject. The passage of time has certainly made such attacks more difficult, but not impossible. The replacement of analog landlines with digital requires an adversary to purchase equipment capable of decoding the digital signal. Weak cryptographic algorithms, such as COMP128 discussed in Chapter 4, prevent simple radios from intercepting calls, but are easily circumvented by only slightly greater sophistication. However, without proximity to a target or physical access to the proprietary equipment of the phone company, successfully eavesdropping on specific individuals is difficult for most would-be attackers. Note that while the latter has occurred recently [141], the compromise of phone network elements is thus far exceedingly rare.

Communications using VoIP are also vulnerable to eavesdropping. Unencrypted SIP sessions occurring over a local area network can be sniffed and recorded using a number of widely available applications (e.g., Wireshark [53], Oreka [36]). The nature of the Internet also increases the odds of interception. While calls in cellular networks or the PSTN are frequently involve more than one provider, the vast majority of calls do not pass through more than two

---

[4] Readers interested in how legal wiretapping actually occurs (and fails) are encouraged to read the work by Sherr et al [165].

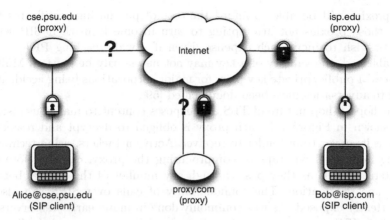

Fig. 7.4. SIPS uses TLS to secure SIP sessions. However, the protection is hop-to-hop between proxies. Accordingly, each proxy has the opportunity to intercept a conversation. The hop-by-hop nature of TLS also prevents a client from preventing colluding intermediate proxies from not using TLS.

domains. Packet traffic, however, is likely to traverse multiple autonomous systems and service providers before being delivered to its final destination. Basic probability, coupled with the fact that the average adversary is more likely to possess the tools necessary to sniff IP packets than the equipment needed to arbitrarily plug into a phone network, make the dangers of unencrypted VoIP traffic all the more real.

In this section, we examine the more widespread security solutions for SIP. We discuss how each solution addresses specific threats and fails to meet others. We then examine threats to IP telephony that currently used encryption protocols do not address.

7.6.1 Current Solutions

SIPS

Realizing the obvious potential for eavesdropping, the base SIP standard contains an option securing IP telephony. Secure SIP (SIPS) protects the confidentiality and integrity of all content sent between a SIP client and its proxy using Transport Layer Security (TLS) [157]. Invocation of SIPS is simple – the protocol portion of an intended recipient's URI is simply appended with the letter "s" (i.e., `sip:bob@isp.com` → `sips:bob@isp.com`). By invoking SIPS, a passive adversary on the path between the sender, intermediate proxies and the receiver are unable to listen in upon calls[5].

There are a number of cases in which SIPS is not sufficient. The lack of a comprehensive PKI may limit a participant's ability to use TLS. While

---

[5] Assuming, of course, that cryptographic keys and certificates are used correctly

most proxies will be able to afford the cost of purchasing certificates from a CA, those proxies not attempting to earn income from their SIP service may not wish to incur such expense. Even if a wide-reaching PKI were to be established, the validity of a key may not necessarily be trusted. Multiple instances of public/private key pairs for major corporations being accidentally issued to adversaries have been documented [59].

The hop-by-hop nature of TLS also exposes content to malicious insiders. As is shown in Figure 7.4, each proxy is obliged to decrypt and re-encrypt traffic as it moves from sender to receiver. Active attackers, using techniques ranging from legal wiretaps to compromising the proxy, can therefore simply intercept calls as they pass through any number of the proxies between source and destination. The confidentiality of calls over SIPS can also be inadvertently exposed. As was commonly done in many early webservers, intermediate SIP proxies may opt to not encrypt outgoing packets (i.e., use the NULL Cipher). Sending unencrypted traffic between proxies may occur in scenarios where proxies are connected by a "trusted network" [6] or simply to increase capacity during busy hours. Regardless of the motivation, failing to re-encrypt SIP traffic between proxies may allow passive adversaries to once again intercept conversations.

SRTP/SRTCP

End-to-end cryptographic protection of SIP calls is possible using *Secure RTP* (SRTP) and *Secure RTCP* (SRTCP) [39]. This pair of protocols provides a framework facilitating the protection of client's calls. To provide confidentiality, SRTP/SRTCP use the *Advanced Encryption Standard* (AES) algorithm running in one of two stream ciphermodes (Counter and f-8 modes) at the call's source and destination. Integrity guarantees are available using the HMAC-SHA1 algorithm. While the use of other algorithms is technically possible, the standards currently only support the above predefined encryption and integrity protections.

There are two noteworthy challenges to the security of sessions running SRTP/SRTCP - use of the NULL cipher and key management. Because only integrity protection is mandated by SRTP/SRTCP, it is possible for clients to knowingly (or otherwise) transmit unencrypted conversations. Without the use of careful checking or network auditing tools (e.g., Wireshark [53]), the leakage of confidential information may be possible even when using SRTP/SRTCP. The key management problem is much more significant. The SRTP/SRTCP standards assume that legitimate participants in a session possess a pre-shared master key, which is used to generate unique session keys

---

[6] "Trusted network" is an overloaded term. For some, this means a network in which all connections are protected by IPsec tunnels. For others, this simply means that all traffic flows through nodes controlled by a single provider. There is typically no reason to believe that the second case provides any real security.

for each call. Given the ability of users to be mobile across both domains and devices, pre-shared private keys are not likely to always be within a user's reach. While key distribution protocols including MIKEY [33] and SDES [31] are suggested, both solutions rely upon the presence of a PKI. The problems inherent to PKIs therefore apply to systems implementing SRTP/SRTCP if these key distribution mechanisms are used.

ZRTP

Recognizing the problems posed by key management in SRTP/SRTCP, the *Media Path Key Agreement for Secure RTP* (ZRTP) attempts to involve the participants of a conversation in key establishment [202]. ZRTP uses a Diffie-Hellman exchange to allow clients to establish a session key for use with SRTP/SRTCP. Unlike the key establishment protocols suggested in the previous section, however, establishing trust in the session key is not dependent on the presence of a PKI. Instead, sender and receiver phones display a short authentication string, which is the result of an HMAC operation. Through the voice channel, both sender and receiver confirm the contents of the string. If an adversary has intercepted their key exchange and altered the session key via man-in-the-middle attack, these strings will not match.

At the time of this writing, the standardization of ZRTP is only in an early phases. Accordingly, details of the protocol are likely to be altered over the coming years. Until such time when it reaches status as an RFC, its deployment is likely to be largely limited.

IPsec

As discussed in Chapter 2, IPsec [107] provides security at the network-layer. IPsec can be configured to ensure confidentiality and/or integrity to higher level services. For instance, an IPsec tunnel can conceal not only the content exchanged between two endpoints, but also the specific processes exchanging that content. While configuring these and other options for IPsec presents its own sets of challenges, the implications of how IPsec is used to provide security for Internet telephony are more significant in this context.

IPsec is often configured to operate in an end-to-end fashion. Specifically, the cryptographic guarantees provided on each packet are only beneficial to the endpoints. For instance, if cryptographic integrity is provided, proxies in between a source and destination have no ability to verify a packet's correctness. Perhaps more critically, end-to-end encryption using IPsec prevents a provider from accessing both the conversation and billing information for a VoIP call. A number of alternative approaches therefore exist. Multi-layered IPsec protocols [201, 49], which encrypt content and information for network proxies using different keys, can satisfy some of the above concerns. Persistent IPsec tunnels can instead be used to protect traffic between proxies. Such a strategy is currently planned for core network components within third generation cellular networks. Much like SIPS, however, this approach provides no guarantees to end hosts about the confidentiality of their calls when inside the provider's proxies.

Even with the above issues worked out, performance still remains a concern when using IPsec. The multi-layered approach described above only adds to the overhead. While dedicated hardware significantly improves the delay associated with this protocol, most users perform the associated cryptographic operations in software. Accordingly, deploying IPsec to provide security for VoIP systems must be done with the utmost consideration and planning.

7.6.2 Analysis of Emerging Vulnerabilities

Cryptography provides a number of valuable tools for the protection of VoIP. Encryption allows sender and receiver to protect the confidentiality of a conversation. Authentication provides assurance that parties involved in a call are indeed who they claim to be. Integrity protections ensure that the fidelity of a call is maintained. However, even in the presence of some of the above security mechanisms, VoIP faces a number of significant threats. We highlight a number of the most serious vulnerabilities revealed in recent research and discuss their implications on the overall security of VoIP.

Attacks On Billing

Billing services are the operational keystone for any commercial VoIP provider. Based on SIP signaling messages, billing allows a provider to charge their customers for delivered services. Without accuracy in billing, however, a company may lose untold revenue. In the absence of integrity and in the presence of fraudulent charges, a provider would likely lose customers to better managed competition. Recognizing this, Zhang et al [200] discovered and confirmed the existence of four significant vulnerabilities in VoIP billing systems. These weaknesses are largely the result of the incorrect or incomplete use of cryptographic protections.

A client using the AT&T SIP network initiates a call by sending an INVITE message to the proxy server. The proxy responds with a request for authentication so as to bill the appropriate client. The client then responds with the appropriate credentials, which are encrypted to prevent eavesdropping. However, because only the credentials are protected, it is possible for a passive adversary to intercept and later replay the credentials. Moreover, because the session descriptor (see Section 7.2.2) is not protected, the adversary can use the stolen credentials to call any number.

A "man in the middle" can intercept a paid phone call in additional ways. After a client transmits its credentials during call establishment, the adversary can return a forged busy signal. This unauthenticated signaling message causes the caller to hang-up while allowing the man in the middle to continue the session at the caller's expense. Alternatively, such an adversary can selectively drop or delay certain types of packets such as BYE messages without detection. Encrypting signaling between clients and proxies offers some protection in that specific types of messages are more difficult to intercept; however, because signaling happens infrequently during a conversation (typically at the beginning and end), context may be a sufficient means of uncovering the meaning of a specific message. Accordingly, cryptographic mechanisms offer little real protection against message dropping attacks.

Tracking Anonymous VoIP

Peer-to-peer VoIP calls offer a number of security properties not found in traditional telephone systems. End-to-end encryption, for example, can protect the contents of a discussion from all but the source and intended destination of a call. As noted in Chapter 2, simply observing packets flow between a source and destination leaks information. Such traffic analysis attacks have already been proven as powerful tools in uncovering complex social relationships and networks known as *Communities of Interest* (COI) in traditional phone [55], data [121] and email [100] networks. Accordingly, traffic analysis attacks represent a serious potential threat to VoIP users if knowledge of a conversation being held must remain confidential.

A simple way to combat this threat is through the use of low-latency anonymization network [76, 177]. Such systems typically forward packets through multiple intermediate hops before ultimately delivering them to their intended destination. While transiting these anonymizing networks, the contents of each packet are typically wrapped in multiple layers of encryption such that an adversary at any point in the network learns only the previous and next hop and noting about the source and destination.

A number of researchers have noted potential attacks on anonymity in such systems. Wright et al [198] investigate how a completely passive adversary can increase their ability to trace the ultimate source and destination of traffic flowing through an anonymizing network. Specifically, these researchers demonstrated that an adversary can significantly improve the probability of determining such information through the compromise of specific individual or sets nodes in the network. Wang et al [191, 192] and Yu et al [199] examine how an active attacker can use a number of techniques including inter-packet spacing to track anonymous VoIP flows. By encoding a hash value in the time between arriving packets, an adversary at both sides of the anonymizing network can confirm the source and destination nodes involved in a conversation. While mechanisms that alter the traffic through anonymizing networks including packet splitting and chaffing can reduce the success of these attacks, simply increasing the time the flow is observed is a sufficient means of combating such defenses. Accordingly, guaranteeing the anonymity of VoIP calls remains an open research problem.

Recovering Language From Encrypted VoIP

When applying well-known, publicly vetted encryption algorithms to data, users expect the resulting contents to be indistinguishable from random bits. However, depending on how they are applied to real systems, even the best encryption algorithms can leak potentially sensitive information to an eavesdropper. Such subtle interplay between the components of the system is what makes systems security so difficult in general.

Wright et al [197] show that a traffic analysis attack on encrypted VoIP sessions can reveal the language spoken by the involved participants. Many VoIP software suites, like cellular phones, use PCM encoders (see Chapter 3 for details on PCM encoding) to transform voice conversations into data streams. Unlike their cellular counterparts, however, many VoIP encoders use variable bitrate schemes so as to minimize the bandwidth used for communication. Accordingly, the data streams resulting from voice encoding contain variably sized packets based on the sounds made by the speaker. While methods such as SRTP protect the actual contents of each individual packet, the use of stream ciphers maintains the size of each of the encrypted packets. Because languages typically possess significantly different packet-length profiles when encoded, it becomes possible to determine the language spoken in an encrypted conversation with as high as 90% accuracy. More recently, the same authors demonstrated the ability to extract specific phrases from encrypted VoIP calls [196].

Preventing the leakage of such information is not as straight-forward as expected. The standards documents for SRTP, for instance, do not provide a block cipher alternative. While such an algorithm could certainly be provided, compliance across different phones may make communication difficult or impossible. Adding padding to each packet may also not prevent this kind of leakage. Specifically, the authors demonstrated that padding all packets to 192 and 256-bit blocks still made it possible to identify the language used in an encrypted conversation with a probability of five times more than randomly guessing. Short of uniform padding of all blocks, which may cause a significant increase in the bandwidth required to conduct such a call, padding is not an entirely effective defense against such an attack. Constant bitrate PCM encoders, such as those used in GSM systems, could provide such a mechanism.

Malware

The application of strong encryption algorithms solves many of the security challenges facing modern communications systems. Even in the presence of the abovementioned information leakages, it is extremely unlikely that an adversary will be able to directly recover the full contents of an encrypted VoIP conversation through a brute force attack on ciphertext within the foreseeable future. In spite of such a strong statement, attacks recovering encrypted

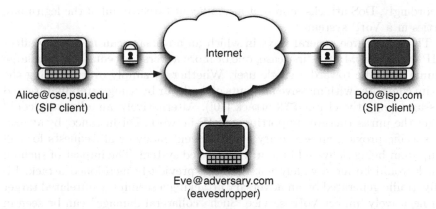

Fig. 7.5. Even in the presence of properly functioning encryption protocols such as SIPS, an adversary can eavesdrop on VoIP calls by compromising a targeted machine. Here, the adversary (Eve) makes Alice's machine forward an unencrypted stream of her conversation in addition to the encrypted version sent to Bob.

VoIP calls are possible today. Specifically, the current state of systems and software security is in such a state of peril that an adversary's most successful strategy for eavesdropping on a conversation would likely be through device compromise.

Malware therefore represents one of the most significant security issues facing VoIP. Any vulnerable piece of software running on a computer used to make VoIP calls is a potential portal through which an adversary can eavesdrop. VoIP software itself may instead be directly targeted. For instance, a number of instances of maliciously modified Skype clients [115, 86] have already been documented. Without careful verification of the software running on and constant vigilance over the integrity of one's system, an attacker may be able to circumvent all of the protections assumed to be in place.

Traditional computing resources are not the only VoIP platforms at risk of compromise. Mobile phones, whether they support both traditional or Internet-based telephony, are also vulnerable to such attacks [82]. As the popularity and ability of such devices continues to grow, so too does the number of exploits [62, 65, 66].

Denial of Service

Simply preventing individuals from communicating represents a powerful tool in an adversary's arsenal. From the perspective of individual VoIP customers, such Denial of Service (DoS) attacks may delay important business transactions or impede emergency officials from responding to calls for assistance. For VoIP providers, such attacks mean that fewer revenue-generating phone calls can be placed, thereby directly impacting a targeted network's earnings.

Accordingly, DoS attacks represent a significant threat to all of the legitimate parties in a VoIP system.

There are three general ways in which an adversary can negatively affect VoIP availability. In the first case, one or more adversaries could direct a large volume of traffic toward a single user. Whether by simply overwhelming the victim computer with massive amounts of traffic or by using carefully targeted messages (e.g., the classic SYN attack [40]). Alternatively, an adversary could target the infrastructure supporting a VoIP network. For instance, by attacking specific proxies, an adversary could prevent many or all requests for call setup from being delivered in a provider-based system. The impact of such an attack would be more widely felt than the previously mentioned attack. Finally, traffic generated by an adversary attacking a seemingly unrelated target can negatively impact VoIP service. Such "collateral damage" can be seen in routers through which attack traffic targeted at one domain and regular traffic for a second domain flows. An adversary attacking a domain receiving service from AT&T may unintentionally degrade the quality of service experienced by AT&T VoIP customers.

Such attacks are, of course, not simply a threat to VoIP telephony. Chapters 5 and 6 investigate low-bandwidth DoS attacks in cellular networks. Significant work on this topic, ranging from classification [122] to mitigation [160, 96, 108] and elimination [102, 193], has also occurred in the Internet domain. However, none of the above techniques have been widely implemented in either voice or data networks. Accordingly, any new application built upon the current communications infrastructure must be aware of the potential for such attacks.

7.7 Building Secure IP Telephony Networks

Standards are offered by the NSA and NIST to help guide those interested in building such systems [113, 132]. However, many challenges remain. For instance, many of the problems discussed in this chapter have fundamentally not been solved by currently available mechanisms. While the use of suggested "best-practices" will certainly decrease the ability of an adversary, significant research toward making more secure networks will be necessary for VoIP telephony systems to reach the same availability guarantees achieved in traditional telephone networks.

Chief to addressing these threats is defining appropriate threat models. As discussed in Chapter 2, a clear understanding of the security challenges facing any network is necessarily the first step in approaching such a problem. Like traditional data traffic, the appropriate application of cryptographic techniques addresses many of the issues of integrity and confidentiality. The real-time requirements of VoIP traffic, however, may or may not be consistently achievable using the public Internet. Depending on how the service is advertised, the tradeoffs between P2P SIP and IMS systems should be considered.

Understanding the threats facing a network and designing accordingly should take a significant effort. There are simply no easy answers to the question of how to build a secure network.

7.8 Summary

In this chapter, we presented a variety of Voice over IP (VoIP) telephony systems and the threats to their secure operation. Our discussion began by examining the evolution of H.323 and the Session Initiation Protocol (SIP), the dominant protocols in the field. Because of its widespread use and rising stature, we explored the architecture, message structure and session establishment process of SIP in depth. Our focus then shifted to next generation telecommunications networks implementing IMS and included a discussion of the tradeoffs associated with infrastructure versus P2P implementations of SIP. We then examined the challenges facing packet-based voice delivery when transmitted using an array of current and future wireless data interfaces.

With an understanding of the architectural and procedural issues affecting VoIP, we then examined the security of such systems. A wide array of protocols, protecting traffic at both the network and transport layers, were then reviewed and compared. Significant weaknesses in these mechanisms in both the P2P and provider assisted settings were noted. Finally, we briefly explored how secure VoIP systems can be constructed.

Because of the significant efficiency gain of packet switching over circuit switching, the use and influence of VoIP will only continue to grow. As these systems become more widely deployed, significant research must be conducted to understand and address the threats these new systems will face.

Part III

Future Analyses

8

Future Directions and Challenges

While informal evidence and conversations indicate that some of the attacks discussed in this book have happened, albeit on a very small scale, most[1] telecommunications systems are thus far fortunate to not have been successfully attacked by a determined adversary. However, the response to such a statement should not ignore the problems presented in this book. The preceding chapters have discussed a number of well-known and emerging threats ton telecommunications networks, many of which are deeply rooted in the architecture of the networks themselves. The continued race toward the convergence of cellular networks and the Internet will therefore only cement the inevitability of such attacks. The lessons learned from this work are not all negative. They give us perspective on design decisions pertinent to all communications networks. They offer us real examples from real systems where optimization permits behavior capable of destabilizing an entire network. Most critically, they remind us that most networks are not truly isolated and will be impacted by the design decisions made by neighboring systems.

In this final chapter, we discuss the lessons learned with regard to rigidity's impact on security. As we will demonstrate, the implications of this work reach far beyond the domain of cellular networks. Finally, because this work illustrates the need for independent evaluations of such systems, we conclude with a discussion on the next steps to be taken in cellular network security research.

8.1 Denial of Service Attacks

8.1.1 Logical vs Flooding Attacks

If the text messaging attack presented in Chapter 5 was categorized immediately after its publication, it almost certainly would have been identified as

---

[1] A recent example of where attackers have been successful is given by Prevelakis et al [141].

a flooding DoS attack. Certainly, our initial understanding and description of the problem would logically have led to such a conclusion - a handful of channels with 762 bits/sec of capacity are connected more or less directly to the Internet. Clearly these channels must have been inundated by the flood of targeted traffic. As it turns out, these channels were overwhelmed, but not in the manner we expected.

The network characterization and mitigation techniques presented throughout Chapter 5 hinted at a flaw in our reasoning. Imagine competition in a traditional data network between two packets. We use a simple model of a single egress queue to clearly illustrate the problem. Assuming that one packet arrives slightly after the other, the longest amount of time this second packet will have to wait is the time it takes to send a *Maximum Transmission Unit* (MTU) sized packet. Accordingly, we can characterize the atomic unit or "channel" size in traditional networks as a single packet. The same, however, is not true in a cellular network. Given a single SDCCH, no amount of multiplexing is possible, even if that SDCCH is not used during a timeslot. The same is true in the assignment of TFIs/TBFs in cellular data networks. The size of the channel in this case is therefore significantly larger than in data networks. Accordingly, every packet originating from a data network must be expanded to the minimum channel size of the cellular network.

This automatic amplification of traffic represents a logical weakness in the protocols of cellular networks. Because some of the time when such channels are held is not used to transmit (i.e., waiting for a response), an adversary attacking such a system exhausts the number of channels and not the bandwidth itself. This argument is made even more clear in Chapter 6, where we demonstrated that the presence of infinite bandwidth does little to improve resiliency against such attacks.

Some logical DoS attacks are relatively simple to fix after they are discovered. Buffer overflow vulnerabilities, for example, can be patched in new versions of code. However, most of the examples from this class of vulnerabilities are deeply rooted within the architecture itself. The attacks discussed in this book are of this sort. Unlike flooding DoS attacks, where bandwidth and processing can be added to protect a system, fundamental changes in the way cellular networks deal with data flows must occur to really address these problems.

8.1.2 Problems in "Controlled" Networks

Many argue that it is the very architecture of the Internet that enables DoS attacks to occur. Routers within the core forward packets without any consideration for the capabilities of their intended endpoints, relegating flow control to an end-to-end issue. Moreover, because packets cross through numerous autonomous systems in their journey between source and destination, acting against DoS attacks upstreams is difficult or impossible. Systems with centralized control like cellular networks, as the argument goes, surely would not experience such problems. With the flick of a switch, a single administrator could easily shut down such attacks. Unfortunately, the reality is far from that simple.

For the above centralized control to be effective, an administrator would need access to an accurate source of global information in real-time. Every component in the network would therefore need to keep the administrator constantly updated with their condition. Such techniques are in fact applied for *call-gapping* overload controls in the PSTN. In particular, if a high-traffic telephony event is known about prior to its occurrence (e.g., concert tickets going on sale), controls can be set to drop some percentage of such requests and respond with a fast busy. These controls allow calls requiring the use of the same switches as the inundated service to be delivered at or near expected rates. While nodes in cellular networks do in fact send status messages to a variety of other points within the network, the information provided in such messages is far from exhaustive. Because conditions can change so quickly, the frequency with which such information would have to be transmitted back to the administrator would require a staggering amount of bandwidth. More-over, after this information arrived and was eventually processed, conditions that caused an alarm may have passed. Like all solutions requiring global knowledge, this problem becomes increasingly difficult to address as a network grows large and mobile. Dealing with low-rate DoS attacks makes this problem even more acute as the boundary between proper, blocking-free operation and an attack is extremely small in these networks. For example, simply changing the profile of an attack from constant rate to pulses of traffic may cause centralized controls to thrash and needlessly restrict the flow of traffic.

It should also be noted that completely controlled networks only exist in the abstract. The vast expansion of inter-connectivity with other service providers, increased functionality of end devices and the addition of new services to such systems obscure the behavior and even the origin of traffic. As cellular providers evolve into common carriers, the ability to truly control and reason about traffic will be significantly reduced.

8.2 End-To-End Arguments and Security

As was true when the End-To-End principle was first published, functionality should not be built into locations and layers where not all traffic can benefit. While previous work has suggested that such functionality may limit scalability and decrease performance, some of the attacks in this book have shown that such practices can actually result in the unexpected failure of the network itself. In so doing, this work raises a number of new observations.

One of the subtle implications of the original End-To-End principal was negatively effecting traffic from neighboring domains. A domain specializing in transporting certain types of traffic, namely those of interest to its business, would likely be less concerned with providing optimizations for traffic passing through the system. Such self-interest could lead to significant problems for clients with traffic traversing multiple domains. In an interesting twist, this work demonstrates that perhaps the inverse is true. By specializing for one type of traffic, a network may actually make itself vulnerable to the traffic generated by its neighbors. However, such a result should not come as a surprise - by ignoring environmental information, in this case traffic from another domain, the system fails to consider a potentially crucial input.

The problems created by one-sided optimizations create concern over the current "net-neutrality" debate. Attempting to provide services instead of just bandwidth, a large number of companies have argued that they should be able to tailor their network to better support their interests. In so doing, certain types of traffic may be treated differently than others. While quality of service mechanisms in the evolving IP standard [175] also attempt to achieve differentiated services, building domain-unique optimizations into each network *may* be dangerous. Such optimizations require reexamination of discussion on active networking by Reed et al [147], in which the authors note that such non-uniform functionality built into lower layers may obscure our understanding not only of traffic in such networks, but also increase the complexity of routing and decimate performance. While this book does not specifically address these issues directly, the impact of rigidity on cellular networks should serve as a design warning.

8.3 The Future of Rigid Systems

Specialization and the rigidity that results from it have their place in some scenarios. Any system with a well defined and limited scope of duties and inputs can in fact benefit from specialization. In a world of technology in which many services attempt to provide every possible function while doing none of them well, specialization can provide truly exceptional systems. Voice-only cellular telecommunications networks are one of the best examples. These systems have long been among the most reliable ever constructed. By leveraging more than a century of telephony experience, these systems provide one of the most efficient and inexpensive means of connecting with the world around us. Rigidity therefore has its place in many systems.

Unfortunately, as these systems have evolved beyond their initial mandate, the rigidity resulting from their specialization poses significant threats to the security of the network. As we have shown in this book, by forcing all flows through such networks to participate in operations optimized for circuit-switched traffic, cellular networks make themselves inherently vulnerable to low-rate denial of service attacks. Using multiple new vulnerabilities, this work has demonstrated that such problems are deeply rooted within the architecture itself and are therefore unlike to be solved quickly.

As we move forward and design new networks, the lessons of rigidity must be remembered. Emerging architectures supporting highly specialized networks should take advantage of optimizations where possible; however, designers must be aware of the complications that may arise when these systems are inter-connected with networks that have fundamentally different requirements and goals. As such system are connected, problems similar to the ones explored in this book will almost certainly reemerge.

8.4 Moving Forward

Both cellular and traditional telecommunications have largely been ignored by the academic security and networking communities. However, these systems have been redesigned and rebuilt many more times than the Internet. Accordingly, such systems must be viewed as an opportunity by researchers - large-scale changes and improvements suggested in this domain may indeed be deployed within the lifetime of their creation.

This book therefore represents only the beginning of the investigation that must occur. Critical high-level areas of analysis include but are by no means limited to:

- **SS7 Security:** Like most legacy technology, the widespread deployment of IMS will not completely replace all SS7 systems. Accordingly, while there are many known security issues in the core of current cellular networks, such systems need additional close analysis.

- **IMS Security:** While these systems are built on IP technology, the challenges these networks will face will be different than the large Internet. Ensuring that such systems are able to meet the performance requirements tasked to real-time communication while fairly delivering best effort traffic will provide sufficient challenges for researchers.

- **SS7/IMS/Internet Convergence:** During the deployment of IMS networks, it is expected that such systems will need to inter-operate with other networks. The implications of these interactions are not well understood and may allow an adversary to disturb traffic across systems.

- **Mobile Device Security:** Mobile device security is very much in its infancy. At the current time, these systems lack the tools necessary to ensure that their interaction with the network are both correct and benign. While device security alone will not solve the problems faced by such networks, it will provide a tremendous tool towards minimizing malicious behavior.

- **Network-based Application Security:** The introduction of an expanding set of services will require continued independent analysis by the security community. Special concerns include not only confidentiality and integrity but also user privacy.

- **Overload Controls:** The move toward common carrier status will force such networks to incorporate more intelligent traffic shaping mechanisms, capable of supporting the demands of various types of traffic (e.g., real time vs. best effort). Properly and efficiently identifying traffic, especially in the presence of encryption, at line speed remain open problems.

The future of security research for telecommunications systems is bright. Using the knowledge gained from this book about the kinds of challenges these systems will face, researchers interested in this field should begin their exploration of specific topics in standards documents available from sources including 3GPP [179], 3GPP2 [178], the ITU [90] and, for SIP, the IETF [174]. By discussing discoveries with providers, equipment vendors and regulatory bodies alike, such research will allow the academic community to expand its contributions and provide valuable insights into these complex and growing systems.

Glossary

1G - First Generation
2G - Second Generation
3DES - Triple DES
3G - Third Generation
8PSK - 8-Phase Shift Keying
A3 - Cryptographic Authentication Algorithm
A5 - Encryption Algorithm
A8 - Session Key Generation Algorithm
AES - Advanced Encryption Standard
AGCH - Access Grant Channel
AMPS - Advanced Mobile Phone System
ASN.1 - Abstract Syntax Notation Language
AuC - Authentication Center
BCCH - Broadcast Control Channel
BSS - Base Station Subsystem
BSSAP+ - Base Station System Application Part +
BTS - Base Transceiver Station
CCH - Common Control Channel
CCS - Common Channel Signaling
CDMA - Code-Division Multiple Access
COI - Communities of Interest
CSD - Circuit Switched Data
CSCF - Call Server Control Function
DCA - Direct Channel Allocation
DES - Data Encryption Standard
DoS - Denial of Service
DDoS - Distributed Denial of Service
DMZ - De-Militarized Zone
DTX - Discontinuous Transmission
EDGE - Enhanced Data Rates for GSM Evolution
EGPRS - Enhanced GPRS (a.k.a. EDGE)

EGSM - Extended GSM
EIR - Equipment Identity Register
ESME - External Short Messaging Entity
ESN - Electronic Serial Number
EV-DO - Enhanced Version - Data Optimized
EV-DV - Enhanced Version - Data and Voice
FDMA - Frequency-Division Multiple Access
GGSN - Gateway GPRS Support Node
GPRS - General Packet Radio Service
GSM - Global System for Mobile Communication
GTP - GPRS Tunneling Protocol
HSCSD - High Speed Circuit Switched Data
HLR - Home Location Register
HSN - Hopping Sequence Number
HSS - Home Subscriber Server
IAM - Initial Address Message
IETF - Internet Engineering Task Force
IKE - Internet Key Exchange
IMEI - International Mobile Equipment Identity
IMSI - International Mobile Subscriber Identity
IMS - IP Multimedia Subsystem
IN - Intelligent Network
ISDN - Integrated Services Digital Network
ISUP - ISDN User Part
ITU - International Telecommunications Union
K_c - Symmetric Session Key
K_i - Client Symmetric Key
LA - Location Area
MAP - Mobile Application Part
MAPsec - Mobile Application Part Security
MCEF - Mobile Capacity Exceeded Flag
MD5 - Message Digest algorithm 5
MMS - Multimedia Messaging Service
MMUSIC - Multiparty Multimedia Session Control
MO - Mobile Originated
MS - Mobile Station
MSISDN - Mobile Subscriber Integrated Services Digital Network Number
MSRN - Mobile Station Routing Number
MT - Mobile Terminated
MSC - Mobile Switching Center
MTP - Message Transfer Part
NANP - North American Numbering Plan
NCS - National Communications System
NDS - Network Domain Security
NIST - National Institute of Standards and Technology

NPA - Numbering Plan Area
NSA - National Security Agency
NSP - Network Services Part
NXX - Numbering Plan Exchange
P-TMSI - Packet Temporary Mobile Subscriber Identity
PACCH - Packet Associated Control Channel
PAGCH - Packet Access Grant Channel
PBCCH - Packet Broadcast Control Channel
PCH - Paging Channel
PCM - Pulse Code Modulation
PDCH - Packet Data Channel
PDP - Packet Data Protocol
PDTCH - Packet Data Traffic Channel
PKI - Public Key Infrastructure
PM - Protection Mode
PPCH - Packet Paging Channel
PRACH - Packet Random Access Channel
PSTN - Public Switched Telephone Network
QoS - Quality of Service
RA - Routing Area
RACH - Random Access Channel
RAI - Routing Area Identity
RED - Random Early Detection
RPE-LTE - Regular Pulse Excitation - Long Term Prediction
RTCP - RTP Control Protocol
RTP - Realtime Transport Protocol
SCCP - Signaling Connection Control Point
SCP - Signaling Control Point
SDCCH - Standalone Dedicated Control Channel
SGSN - Serving GPRS Support Node
SHA-1 - Secure Hash Algorithm 1
SID - Silence Descriptor
SIM - Subscriber Identity Module
SIP - Session Initiation Protocol
SIPS - Secure SIP
SMPP - Short Messaging Peer Protocol
SMS - Short Messaging Service
SMSC - Short Messaging Service Center
SRP - Static Resource Provisioning
SRTCP - Secure RTCP
SRTP - Secure RTP
SS7 - Signaling System Number 7
SSL - Secure Sockets Layer
TACS - Total Access Communication System
TBF - Temporary Block Flow

TCAP - Transaction Capabilities Application Part
TCH - Traffic Channel
TDMA - Time-Division Multiple Access
TFI - Temporary Flow Identifier
TMSI - Temporary Mobile Subscriber Identity
TRX - Transmission Channel
UMTS - Universal Mobile Telecommunication System
UHF - Ultra-High Frequency
URI - Uniform Resource Identifier
VAD - Voice Activity Detection
VLR - Visitor Location Register
VoIP - Voice over IP
WCDMA - Wide-band CDMA
WFQ - Weighted Fair Queuing
WRED - Weighted Random Early Detection
ZRTP - Media Path Key Agreement for Secure RTP

References

1. Computer Emergency Response Team. http://www.cert.org/.
2. National Institute of Standards and Technology. http://www.nist.gov/.
3. OpenSSL. http://www.openssl.org/.
4. Young prefer texting to calls'. http://news.bbc.co.uk/2/hi/business/2985072.stm, June 2003.
5. 3G Americas, LLC. 3G Americas::Unifying the Americas through Wireless Technology. http://www.3gamericas.org.
6. 3rd Generation Partnership Project. Comfort Noise Aspects for Full Rate Speech Traffic Channels. Technical Report 3GPP TS 06.12 v8.1.0.
7. 3rd Generation Partnership Project. Discontinuous Transmission (DTX) for Full Rate Speech Traffic Channels. Technical Report 3GPP TS 06.31 v8.0.1.
8. 3rd Generation Partnership Project. Full rate speech; Processing functions . Technical Report 3GPP TS 06.01 v8.0.1.
9. 3rd Generation Partnership Project. Full rate speech; Substitution and muting of lost frames for full rate speech channels. Technical Report 3GPP TS 06.11 v8.0.1.
10. 3rd Generation Partnership Project. Full rate speech; Transcoding. Technical Report 3GPP TS 06.10 v8.2.0.
11. 3rd Generation Partnership Project. General Packet Radio Service (GPRS); Mobile Station (MS) - Base Station System (BSS) interface; Radio Link Control/Medium Access Control (RLC/MAC) protocol. Technical Report 3GPP TS 44.060 v7.6.0.
12. 3rd Generation Partnership Project. General Packet Radio Service (GPRS); Overall description of GPRS radio interface; Stage 2. Technical Report 3GPP TS 03.64 v8.12.0.
13. 3rd Generation Partnership Project. General Packet Radio Service (GPRS); Service description;. Technical Report 3GPP TS 03.60 v7.9.0.
14. 3rd Generation Partnership Project. GSM/EDGE Radio Access Network; General PAcket Radio Service (GPRS); Overall description of the GPRS radio interface; Stage 2. Technical Report 3GPP TS 43.064 v7.2.0.
15. 3rd Generation Partnership Project. Organization of subscriber data. Technical Report 3GPP TS 03.08 v7.5.0.
16. 3rd Generation Partnership Project. Physical layer on the radio path; General description. Technical Report 3GPP TS 05.01 v8.9.0.

17. 3rd Generation Partnership Project. Physical layer on the radio path; General description. Technical Report 3GPP TS 04.18 v8.26.0.

18. 3rd Generation Partnership Project. Radio Access Network; Radio transmission and reception. Technical Report 3GPP TS 05.05 v8.20.0.

19. 3rd Generation Partnership Project. Technical realization of the Short Message Service (SMS). Technical Report 3GPP TS 03.40 v7.5.0.

20. 3rd Generation Partnership Project. Technical Specification Group Core Network and Terminals; Mobile Application Part (MAP) specification. Technical Report 3GPP TS 29.002 v8.1.0.

21. 3rd Generation Partnership Project. Technical Specification Group GSM/EDGE, Radio Access Network; Channel coding. Technical Report 3GPP TS 45.003 v7.1.0.

22. 3rd Generation Partnership Project. Technical Specification Group GSM/EDGE Radio Access Network; Multiplexing and multiple access on the radio path. Technical Report 3GPP TS 05.02 v8.11.0.

23. 3rd Generation Partnership Project. Technical Specification Group Radio Access Network; Medium Access Control (MAC) protocol specification (Release 7). Technical Report 3GPP TS 25.321 v7.2.0.

24. 3rd Generation Partnership Project. Technical Specification Group Services and System Aspects; 3G Security; Network Domain Security; MAP application layer security . Technical Report 3GPP TS 33.200 v7.0.0.

25. 3rd Generation Partnership Project. Technical Specification Group Terminals; Alphabets and language-specific information. Technical Report 3GPP TS 23.038 v7.0.0.

26. 3rd Generation Partnership Project. Voice Activity Detection (VAD). Technical Report 3GPP TS 06.32 v8.0.1.

27. A. Abutaleb and V. O. Li. Paging strategy optimization in personal communication systems. *Wireless Networks*, 3(3):195–204, 1997.

28. American District Telegraph (ADT). Frequently Asked Questions (FAQ's). http://www.adt.com/wps/portal/adt/customer_service/?wgc= for_your_home/cellular_radio_monitoring_faqs, 2007.

29. P. Amrein. BMD Wireless Announces Commercial Availability of Application SMSC and High Speed Messaging Platform. http://www.intradoemea.com/main.php?content=newsflash_08200201, 2002.

30. R. Anderson. Usenet Group uk.telecom: A5 (Was: HACKING DIGITAL PHONES). http://groups.google.com/group/uk.telecom/msg/ba76615fef32ba32, 1994.

31. F. Andreasen, M. Baugher, and D. Wing. RFC 4568: Session Description Protocol (SDP) Security Descriptions for Media Streams. http://tools.ietf.org/html/rfc4568, 2006.

32. Antenna Systems & Solutions, Inc. Tactical Response Cell Phone Jammer (TRJ) - Antenna Systems & Solutions. www.antennasystems.com/cellular/trj-89_cellphonejammer.htm, 2008.

33. J. Arkko, E. Carrara, F. Lindholm, M. Naslund, and K. Norrman. RFC 3830: MIKEY: Multimedia Internet KEYing. http://tools.ietf.org/html/rfc3830, 2004.

34. A. Arpaci-Dusseau and R. Arpaci-Dusseau. Information and Control in Gray-Box Systems. In *Proceedings of Symposium on Operating Systems Principles (SOSP)*, 2001.

35. AT&T Wireless. Picture & Video Messaging and Frequently asked questions. http://www.wireless.att.com/learn/messaging-internet/messaging/faq-multimedia-messaging.jsp, 2007.

36. Audacity Development Team. Oreka: Audio streams recording and retrieval. http://oreka.sourceforge.net/, 2007.

37. S. Axelsson. The Base-Rate Fallacy and its Implications for the Difficulty of Intrusion Detection. *Proceedings of the 6th ACM Conference on Computer and Communications Security*, 1999.

38. E. Barkhan, E. Biham, and N. Keller. Instant Ciphertext-Only Cryptanalysis of GSM Encrypted Communication. In *Proceedings of the Annual International Cryptology Conference (CRYPTO)*, 2003.

39. M. Baugher, D. McGrew, M. Naslund, E. Carrara, and K. Norrman. RFC 3711: The Secure Real-time Transport Protocol (SRTP). http://tools.ietf.org/html/rfc3711, 2004.

40. S. Bellovin. Security problems in the TCP/IP protocol suite. *Computer Communications Review*, 19(2):32–48, April 1989.

41. E. Biham and O. Dunkelman. Cryptanalysis of the A5/1 GSM Stream Cipher. In *Proceedings of INDOCRYPT*, 2000.

42. E. Biham, O. Dunkelman, and N. Keller. A Related-Key Rectangle Attack on the Full KASUMI. In *Proceedings of ASIACRYPT*, 2005.

43. A. Biryukov, A. Shamir, and D. Wagner. Real Time Cryptanalysis of A5/1 on a PC. In *Proceedings of the Fast Software Encryption Workshop*, 2000.

44. B. Branden, D. Clark, J. Crowcroft, B. Davie, S. Deering, D. Estrin, S. Floyd, V. Jacobson, G. Minshall, C. Partridge, L. Peterson, K. Ramakrishnan, S. Shenker, J. Wroclawski, and L. Zhang. RFC 2309: Recommendations on Queue Management and congestion Avoidance in the Internet. http://tools.ietf.org/html/rfc2309, 1998.

45. S. Buckingham. What is GPRS? http://www.gsmworld.com/technology/gprs/intro.shtml#5, 2000.

46. N. Burnett, J. Bent, A. Arpaci-Dusseau, and R. Arpaci-Dusseau. Exploiting Gray-Box Knowledge of Buffer-Cache Management. In *Proceedings of USENIX Annual Technical Conference*, 2002.

47. R. Buskey, H. Chen, T. La Porta, J. Larson, S. Mizikovsky, and P. Traynor. Cellular Networks Security Panel. USENIX Security Symposium, 2007.

48. S. Byers, A. Rubin, and D. Kormann. Defending Against an Internet-based Attack on the Physical World. *ACM Transactions on Internet Technology (TOIT)*, 4(3):239–254, August 2004.

49. H. Choi, H. Song, G. Cao, and T. La Porta. Mobile Multi-Layered IPsec. In *Proceedings of IEEE INFOCOM*, 2005.

50. A. Choong. Wireless Watch: Jammed. http://asia.cnet.com/reviews/handphones/wirelesswatch/0,39020107,39186280,00.htm, September 7, 2004.

51. Cisco Systems Whitepaper. A study in mobile messaging: The evolution of messaging in mobile networks, and how to efficiently and effectively manage the growing messaging traffic. Technical report, 2004.

52. D. Clark, J. Wroslawski, K. Sollins, and R. Braden. Tussle in Cyberspace: Defining Tomorrow's Internet. In *Proceedings of ACM SIGCOMM*, 2002.

53. G. Combs. Wireshark. http://www.wireshark.org/, 2007.

54. Computer Security: Art and Science. *Matt Bishop*. Addison-Wesley, Reading, MA, 2003.

55. C. Cortes, D. Pregibon, and C. Volinsky. Communities of Interest. In *Proceedings of the International Conference on Advances in Intelligent Data Analysis (IDA)*, 2001.

56. Cryptome. Interception of GSM Cellphones. http://cryptome.org/gsm-spy.htm, 2005.

57. A. Demers, S. Keshav, and S. Shenker. Analysis and Simulation of a Fair Queueing Algorithm. In *Proceedings of ACM SIGCOMM*, pages 3–12, 1989.

58. D. Eastlake and P. Jones. US Secure Hash Algorithm 1 (SHA1). Internet Engineering Task Force RFC 3174, Sept. 2001.

59. C. M. Ellison and B. Schneier. Ten Risks of PKI: What You're Not Being Told About Public-Key Infrastructure. *Computer Security Journal*, 16(1):1–7, 1999.

60. J. Elwell. RFC 4916: Connected Identity in the Session Initiation Protocol (SIP). http://tools.ietf.org/html/rfc4916, 2007.

61. W. Enck, P. Traynor, P. McDaniel, and T. F. La Porta. Exploiting Open Functionality in SMS-Capable Cellular Networks. In *Proceedings of the ACM Conference on Computer and Communication Security (CCS)*, November 2005.

62. F-Secure Corporation. F-Secure Virus Descriptions : Cabir.H. http://www.f-secure.com/v-descs/cabir_h.shtml, December 2004.

63. F-Secure Corporation. F-Secure Virus Descriptions : Duts.1520. http://www.f-secure.com/v-descs/dtus.shtml, 2004.

64. F-Secure Corporation. F-Secure Virus Descriptions : Commwarrior. http://www.f-secure.com/v-descs/commwarrior.shtml, 2005.

65. F-Secure Corporation. F-Secure Virus Descriptions : Mabir.A. http://www.f-secure.com/v-descs/mabir.shtml, April 2005.

66. F-Secure Corporation. F-Secure Virus Descriptions : Skulls.A. http://www.f-secure.com/v-descs/skulls.shtml, January 2005.

67. D. Farber, L. Dignan, and D. Berlind. Why the FCC's 700Mhz auction matters. http://blogs.zdnet.com/BTL/?p=5807, 2007.

68. Federal Communications Commission. Year 2000 Biennial Review Amendment of Part 22 of the Commissions Rules to Modify or Eliminate Outdated Rules Affecting the Cellular Radiotelephone Service and Other Commercial Mobile Radio Service, 2000.

69. Federal Communications Commission. FCC: Wireless Services: Broadband PCS: Operations: Blocking & Jamming. http://wireless.fcc.gov/services/index.htm?job=operations_1&id=broadband_pcs, 2002.

70. Federal Communications Commission. Auction 73: 700 MHz Band. http://wireless.fcc.gov/auctions/default.htm?job=auction_summary&id=73, 2008.

71. S. Floyd and V. Jacobson. Random Early Detection Gateways for Congestion Avoidance. *IEEE/ACM Transactions on Networking*, 1(4):397–413, August 1993.

72. Gateway to Russia. Mobile networks facing overload. http://www.gateway2russia.com/st/art_187902.php, December 31, 2003.

73. General Electric. GE Security. http://www.gesecurity.com/portal/site/GESecurity, 2007.

74. General Motors. OnStar Car Safety Device and Vehicle Security System. http://www.onstar.com, 2007.

75. I. Goldberg, D. Wagner, and M. Briceno. GSM Cloning. http://www.isaac.cs.berkeley.edu/isaac/gsm.html, 1998.

76. D. M. Goldschlag, M. G. Reed, and P. F. Syverson. "Onion Routing for Anonymous and Private Internet Connections. *Communications of the ACM*, 42(2), February 1999.

77. J. D. Golic. Cryptanalysis of Alleged A5 Stream Cipher. In *Proceedings of EuroCrypt*, 1997.

78. M. Grenville. Operators: Celebration Messages Overload SMS Network. http://www.160characters.org/news.php?action=view&nid=819, November 2003.

79. GSM World. Brief History of GSM & the GSMA. http://www.gsmworld.com/about/history.shtml, 2007.

80. GSM World. GSM Operators, Coverage Maps and Roaming Information - Countries/Areas. http://www.gsmworld.com/roaming/gsminfo/index.shtml, 2007.

81. GSM World. GSM Security Algorithms. http://www.gsmworld.com/using/algorithms/index.shtml, 2008.

82. C. Guo, H. J. Wang, and W. Zhu. Smart Phone Attacks and Defenses. In *Proceedings of Third ACM Workshop on Hot Topics in Networks (HotNets-III)*, 2004.

83. D. Hanluain. They Be Jammin' in France. http://www.wired.com/culture/lifestyle/news/2002/03/51273, 2002.

84. D. Harkins and D. Carrel. The Internet Key Exchange. *Internet Engineering Task Force*, November 1998. RFC 2409.

85. Hewlett-Packard. HP to Drive Mobile Connectivity Around the Globe with Vodafone. http://www.hp.com/hpinfo/newsroom/press/2006/060706b.html, 2006.

86. M. Hines. Attackers Get Chatty on VOIP. http://www.pcworld.com/businesscenter/article/132389/attackers_get_chatty_on_voip.html, May 2007.

87. Intel Whitepaper. SMS Messaging in SS7 Networks: Optimizing Revenue with Modular Components. Technical report, 2003.

88. International Electrotechnical Commission. Audio recording - Compact disc digital audio system. Technical Report IEC 60908.

89. International Telecommunications Union. H.261 : Video codec for audiovisual services at p x 64 kbit/s. Technical Report ITU-T Recommendation H.261.

90. International Telecommunications Union. ITU: Committed to connecting the world. http://www.itu.int/.

91. International Telecommunications Union. Narrow-band visual telephone systems and terminal equipment. Technical Report ITU-T Recommendation H.320.

92. International Telecommunications Union. Packet-based multimedia communications systems. Technical Report ITU-T Recommendation H.323.

93. International Telecommunications Union. Pulse code modulation (PCM) of voice frequencies. Technical Report ITU-T Recommendation G.711.

94. International Telecommunications Union. Transmission performance characteristics of pulse code modulation channels. Technical Report ITU-T Recommendation G.712.

95. Internet Engineering Task Force. Session Initiation Protocol (sip). Technical report.

96. J. Ioannidis and S. Bellovin. Implementing Pushback: Router-Based Defense Against DDoS Attacks. In *Proceedings of Network and Distributed System Security Symposium (NDSS)*, February 2002.

97. ITFacts. Mobile Usage: 2.7% of Americans downloaded a mobile game. `http://www.itfacts.biz/index.php?id=P6428`, 2006.

98. iTnews. Record calls, text again expected for NYE. `http://www.itnews.com.au/newsstory.aspx?CIaNID=17434`, December 31, 2004.

99. R. Jain. Myths about congestion management in high speed networks. *Internetworking: Research and Experience*, 3:101–113, 1992.

100. L. Johansen, K. Butler, M. Rowell, and P. McDaniel. Email Communities of Interest. In *Proceedings of the Conference on Email and Anti-Spam (CEAS)*, 2007.

101. D. Johnson, C. Perkins, and J. Arkko. RFC 3775: Mobility Support in IPv6. `http://tools.ietf.org/html/rfc3775`, 2004.

102. A. Juels and J. G. Brainard. Client Puzzles: A Cryptographic Countermeasure Against Connection Depletion Attacks. In *Proceedings of Network and Distributed System Security Symposium (NDSS)*, 1999.

103. D. Kahn. *The Codebreakers*. Macmillan Publishing Co., 1967.

104. C. Kaufman, R. Perlman, and M. Speciner. *Network security: private communication in a public world*. Prentice-Hall, Inc., Upper Saddle River, NJ, USA, 2nd edition, 2002.

105. S. Kent and R. Atkinson. IP Authentication Header. RFC 2402, Nov. 1998.

106. S. Kent and R. Atkinson. IP Encapsulating Security Payload. RFC 2406, Nov. 1998.

107. S. Kent and R. Atkinson. RFC 2401: Security Architecture for the Internet Protocol. `http://tools.ietf.org/html/rfc2401`, 1998.

108. A. Keromytis, V. Misra, and D. Rubenstein. SOS: Secure Overlay Services. In *Proceedings of ACM SIGCOMM*, 2002.

109. G. Kim, S. H. Lee, S. C. Lee, H. G. Lee, and O. Kwon. MONETA Services of SK Telecom: Lessons from Business Convergence Experiences for Ubiqu itous Computing Services. In *Proceedings of the 2nd IEEE Workshop on Software Technologies for Future Embedded and U biquitous Systems (WSTFEUS'04)*, 2004.

110. K. Kotapati, P. Liu, and T. La Porta. CAT - A Practical Graph & SDL Based Toolkit for Vulnerability Assessment of 3G Networks. In *Proceedings of the IFIP International Information Security Conference, Security and Privacy in Dynamic Environments*, 2006.

111. B. Krebs. Research May Hasten Death of Mobile Privacy Standard. `http://blog.washingtonpost.com/securityfix/2008/02/research_may_spell_end_of_mobi.html`, 2008.

112. B. Krishnamachari, R.-H. Gau, S. B. Wicker, and Z. J. Haas. Optimal sequential paging in cellular wireless networks. *Wireless Networks*, 10(2):121–131, 2004.

113. D. R. Kuhn, T. J. Walsh, and S. Fries. Security Considerations for Voice Over IP Systems. Technical Report Special Report 800-58, National Institute of Standards and Technology (NIST), 2005.

114. G. Kunene. Perimeter Security Ain't What It Used to Be, Experts Say. *DevX.com*, 2004.

115. J. LeClaire. Malware Writers Exploit Skype Hype. `http://www.technewsworld.com/story/voip/46802.html`, October 18, 2005.

116. C. Lepschy, G. Minerva, D. Minervini, and F. Pascali. GSM-GPRS radio access dimensioning. In *IEEE Technology Conference (VTC Fall)*, 2001.

117. G. Lorenz, T. Moore, G. Manes, J. Hale, and S. Shenoi. Securing SS7 Telecommunications Networks. In *Proceedings of the IEEE Workshop on Information Assurance and Security*, 2001.

118. Lucent Technologies. 5ESS(R) 2000 - Switch Mobile Switching Centre (MSC) for Service Providers. `http://www.lucent.com/products/solution/0,,CTID+2019-STID+10048-SOID+824-LOCL+1,00.html`, 2006.

119. K. Maney. Surge in text messaging makes cell operators :-). `http://www.usatoday.com/money/2005-07-27-text-messaging_x.htm`, July 27 2005.

120. S. Marwaha. Will Success Spoil SMS? `http://wirelessreview.com/mag/wireless_success_spoil_sms/`, March 15, 2001.

121. P. McDaniel, S. Sen, O. Spatscheck, J. V. der Merwe, B. Aiello, and C. Kalmanek. Enterprise Security: A Community of Interest Based Approach. In *Proceedings of the Network & Distributed System Security Symposium (NDSS)*, 2006.

122. J. Mirkovic and P. Reiher. A Taxonomy of DDoS Attacks and DDoS Defense Mechanisms. *ACM SIGCOMM Computer Communication Review*, 34(2):39–53, 2004.

123. G. S. Mobile. Services and Facilities to be provided in the GSM System. Technical Report GSM Doc 28/85, Revision 2, June 1985.

124. T. Moore, T. Kosloff, J. Keller, G. Manes, and S. Shenoi. Signaling System 7 Network Security. In *Proceedings of the IEEE 45th Midwest Symposium on Circuits and Systems*, 2002.

125. Motorola Corporation. Motorola GSM Solutions. `www.motorola.com/networkoperators/pdfs/GSM-Solutions.pdf`, 2006.

126. C. Mulliner and G. Vigna. Vulnerability Analysis of MMS User Agents. In *Proceedings of the Annual Computer Security Applications Conference (ACSAC)*, 2006.

127. R. Mullner, C. F. Ball, K. Ivanov, and H. Winkler. Advanced quality of service strategies for GERAN mobile radio networks. In *IEEE Symposium on Personal, Indoor and Mobile Radio Communications (PIMRC)*, 2004.

128. J. Nagle. RFC 896: Congestion Control in IP/TCP Internetworks. `http://www.ietf.org/rfc/rfc896.txt`, 1984.

129. J. B. Nagle. On Packet Switches with Infinite Storage. *IEEE Transactions on Communications*, COM-35(4), April 1987.

130. National Bureau of Standards. Data Encryption Standard. *Federal Information Processing Standards Publication*, 1976.

131. National Communications System. SMS over SS7. Technical Report Technical Information Bulletin 03-2 (NCS TIB 03-2), December 2003.

132. National Security Agency. Recommended IP Telephony Architecture. Technical Report I332-009R-2006, Systems and Network Attack Center (SNAC), 2006.

133. P. Neumann. Cause of AT&T network failure. *The Risks Digest*, 9(62), 1990.

134. NIST. Recommendation for the Triple Data Encryption Algorithm (TDEA) Block Cipher. Special Publication 800-67, 2004.

135. Nyquetek, Inc. Wireless Priority Service for National Security. `http://wireless.fcc.gov/releases/da051650PublicUse.pdf`, 2002.

136. J. Pearce. Mobile firms gear up for New Years text-fest. `http://news.zdnet.co.uk/communications/networks/0,39020345,39118812,00.htm`, December 30, 2003.

137. J. Peterson. RFC 3853: S/MIME Advanced Encryption Standard (AES) Requirement for the Session Initiation Protocol (SIP). http://tools.ietf.org/html/rfc3853, 2004.

138. S. Petrovic and A. Fuster-Sabater. An Improved Cryptanalysis of the A5/2 Algorithm for Mobile Communications. In *Proceedings of Communication Systems and Networks*, 2002.

139. Phone Jammer: Cell Phone Jammer Specialists. Cell Phone Jammer, Low Power Mobile Phone Jammers, Blocker Stopper - Buy Here - Cool ! http://phonejammer.com/, 2008.

140. G. Platform. Implementations: Mobile Telecom. http://www.globalplatform.org/, March 2008.

141. V. Prevelakis and D. Spinellis. The Athens Affair. *IEEE Spectrum*, pages 18–25, July 2007.

142. R. Racic, D. Ma, and H. Chen. Exploiting MMS Vulnerabilities to Stealthily Exhaust Mobile Phone's Battery. In *Proceedings of the IEEE International Conference on Security and Privacy in Communication Networks (SecureComm)*, 2006.

143. A. Ramirez. Theft Through Cellular 'Clone' Calls. *The New York Times*, April 7, 1992.

144. J. Rao, P. Rohatgi, H. Scherzer, and S. Tinguely. Partitioning Attacks: Or How to Rapidly Clone Some GSM Cards. In *Proceedings of the IEEE Symposium on Security and Privacy (OAKLAND)*, 2002.

145. M. Reardon. ThinkPads to support Cingular 3G technology. http://news.com.com/ThinkPads+to+support+Cingular+3G+technology/2100-1034_3-6017968.html, 2006.

146. M. Reardon. Sprint unveils WiMax plans. http://www.news.com/Sprint-unveils-WiMax-plans/2100-1039_3-6170672.html, 2007.

147. D. Reed, J. Saltzer, and D. Clark. Active Networking and End-To-End Arguments. *IEEE Network*, 12(3):67–71, May/June 1998.

148. Research In Motion. Blackberry. http://www.blackberry.com/, 2006.

149. F. Ricciato. Unwanted Traffic in 3G Networks. In *ACM SIGCOMM Computer Communication Review*, 2006.

150. M. Richtel. Yahoo Attributes a Lengthy Service Failure to an Attack. *The New York Times*, February 8 2000.

151. M. Richtel. Devices Enforce Silence of Cellphones, Illegally. *The New York Times*, November 4, 2007.

152. R. Rivest. The MD5 Message Digest Algorithm. *Internet Engineering Task Force*, April 1992. RFC 1321.

153. R. Rivest, A. Shamir, and L. Adleman. A Method for Obtaining Digital Signatures and Public-Key Cryptosystems. *Communications of the ACM*, 21(2):120–126, February 1978.

154. A. B. Roach. RFC 3265: Session Initiation Protocol (SIP)-Specific Event Notification. http://tools.ietf.org/html/rfc3265, 2002.

155. Roam Secure. 17 Counties & Cities in Washington, DC Region deploy Roam Secure Alert Network. http://www.roamsecure.net/story.php?news_id=52, September 2005.

156. R. Rosenbaum. Secrets of the Little Blue Box. *Esquire Magazine*, pages 117–125 and 222–226, October 1971.

157. J. Rosenberg, H. Schulzrinne, G. Camarillo, A. Johnston, J. Peterson, R. Sparks, M. Handley, and E. Schooler. RFC 3261: SIP: Session Initiation Protocol. http://tools.ietf.org/html/rfc3261, 2002.

158. J. H. Saltzer, D. P. Reed, and D. D. Clark. End-To-End Arguments In System Design. *ACM Transactions on Computer Systems*, 2(4):277–288, 1984.

159. SANS Institute. The GSM Standard (An Overview of Its Security). http://www.sans.org/rr/papers/index.php?id=317, 2001.

160. S. Savage, D. Wetherall, A. Karlin, and T. Anderson. Practical network support for IP traceback. In *Proceedings of ACM SIGCOMM*, pages 295–306, October 2000.

161. F. B. Schneider, editor. *Trust in Cyberspace*. National Academy Press, 1999.

162. M. Schwartz. Addison-Wesley Publishing Company, 1987.

163. J. Serror, H. Zang, and J. C. Bolot. Impact of paging channel overloads or attacks on a cellular network. In *Proceedings of the ACM Workshop on Wireless Security (WiSe)*, 2006.

164. G. Shannon. Security Vulnerabilities in Protocols. In *Proceedings of ITU-T Workshop on Security*, May 13-14 2002.

165. M. Sherr, E. Cronin, S. Clark, and M. Blaze. Signaling Vulnerabilities in Wiretapping Systems. *IEEE Security & Privacy*, 3(6):13–25, November/December 2005.

166. Skype Limited. Skype - Internet Calls. http://www.skype.com/, 2007.

167. R. Sparks. RFC 4320: Actions Addressing Identified Issues with the Session Initiation Protocol's (SIP) Non-INVITE Transaction. http://tools.ietf.org/html/rfc4320, 2006.

168. S. Staniford, V. Paxson, and N. Weaver. How to Own the Internet in Your Spare Time. In *Usenix Security Symposium*, pages 149–167, 2002.

169. Start Corp. http://www.startcorp.com, 2005.

170. Tamara Neale. VDOT LAUNCHES NEW 511 EMAIL ALERT SERVICE. http://www.virginiadot.org/infoservice/news/newsrelease.asp?ID=CO-511-06, February 2006.

171. S. Telecom. Moneta Stock. http://www.sktelecom.com/, March 2008.

172. Telecommunication Industry Association/Electronic Industries Association (TIA/EIA) Standard. Short Messaging Service for Spread Spectrum Systems. Technical Report ANSI/TIA/EIA-637-A-1999.

173. The 104th Congress of the United States. The Telecommunications Act of 1996. http://www.fcc.gov/Reports/tcom1996.txt, 1996. Pub. LA. No. 104-104.

174. The Internet Engineering Task Force. IETF Home Page. http://www.ietf.org/.

175. The Internet Engineering Task Force. RFC 2460: Internet Protocol, Version 6 (IPv6) Specification. http://www.ietf.org/rfc/rfc2460.txt, 1998.

176. The Signal Jammer. TheSignalJammer.com: Cellular and GPS Jamming Products. http://www.thesignaljammer.com/, 2008.

177. The Tor Project. Tor: anonymity online. http://tor.eff.org/, 2007.

178. Third Generation Partnership Plan 2 (3GPP2). Developing the Next Generation of cdma2000 Wireless Communications. http://www.3gpp2.org.

179. Third Generation Partnership Plan (3GPP). Shaping the future of mobile communication standards. http://www.3gpp.org.

180. Tom's Hardware. How To: Building a BlueSniper Rifle. http://www.tomsnetworking.com/Sections-article106.php, March 2005.

181. P. Traynor. *Characterizing the Impact of Rigidity on the Security of Cellular Telecommunications Networks*. PhD thesis, The Pennsylvania State University, 2008.

182. P. Traynor, W. Enck, P. McDaniel, and T. La Porta. Mitigating Attacks on Open Functionality in SMS-Capable Cellular Networks. In *Proceedings of the Twelfth Annual ACM International Conference on Mobile Computing and Networking (MobiCom)*, 2006.

183. P. Traynor, W. Enck, P. McDaniel, and T. La Porta. Mitigating Attacks on Open Functionality in SMS-Capable Cellular Networks. *IEEE/ACM Transactions on Networking (TON)*, To Appear.

184. P. Traynor, W. Enck, P. McDaniel, and T. La Porta. Exlopiting Open Functionality in SMS-Capable Cellular Networks. *Journal of Computer Security (JCS)*, To Appear 2008.

185. P. Traynor, P. McDaniel, and T. La Porta. On Attack Causality in Internet-Connected Cellular Networks. In *Proceedings of the USENIX Security Symposium*, 2007.

186. P. Traynor, V. Rao, T. Jaeger, P. McDaniel, and T. La Porta. From Mobile Phones to Responsible Devices. Technical Report NAS-TR-0059-2007, Network and Security Research Center, Department of Computer Science and Engineering, Pennsylvania State University, University Park, PA, 2007.

187. Trifinite. BlueBug. http://trifinite.org/trifinite_stuff_bluebug.html, 2004.

188. United States Census Bureau. United States Census 2000. http://www.census.gov/main/www/cen2000.html, 2000.

189. Verizon Wireless. Verizon Wireless Picture & Video Messaging. http://www.vzwpix.com/pri/composer/guestCreate.do?sortField=-creationDate&category=Stuff+to+Send%2CE-Cards, 2007.

190. Vonage Marketing, Inc. Vonage - A Better Phone Service For Less. http://www.vonage.com/, 2007.

191. X. Wang, S. Chen, and S. Jajodia. Tracking Anonymous Peer-to-Peer VoIP Calls on the Internet. In *Proceedings of the ACM Conference on Computer and Communications Security (CCS)*, 2005.

192. X. Wang, S. Chen, and S. Jajodia. Network Flow Watermarking Attack on Low-Latency Anonymous Communication Systems. In *Proceedings of the IEEE Symposium on Security and Privacy (OAKLAND)*, 2007.

193. B. Waters, A. Juels, J. Halderman, and E. Felten. New client puzzle outsourcing techniques for DoS resistance. In *Proceedings of ACM Conference on Computer and Communications Security (CCS)*, pages 246–256, 2004.

194. J. Wexler. WiMax service hits Seattle. http://www.techworld.com/mobility/features/index.cfm?featureid=1434, 2005.

195. WiMAX Forum. Welcome to the WiMAX Forum. http://www.wimaxforum.org/home/, 2007.

196. C. Wright, L. Ballard, S. Coull, F. Monrose, and G. Masson. Spot me if you can: Uncovering spoken phrases in encrypted VoIP conversations. In *Proceedings of IEEE Symposium on Security and Privacy (OAKLAND)*, 2008.

197. C. Wright, L. Ballard, F. Monrose, and G. Masson. Language Identification of Encrypted VoIP Traffic: Alejandra y Roberto or Alice and Bob? In *Proceedings of the USENIX Security Symposium*, 2007.

198. M. Wright, M. Adler, B. N. Levine, and C. Shields. Passive Logging Attacks Against Anonymous Communications. *ACM Transactions on Information and Systems Security (TISSEC)*, To appear, 2008.

199. W. Yu, X. Fu, S. Graham, D. Xuan, and W. Zhao. DSSS-based Flow Marking Technique for Invisible Traceback. In *Proceedings of IEEE Symposium on Security and Privacy (OAKLAND)*, 2007.

200. R. Zhang, X. Wang, X. Yang, and X. Jiang. Billing Attacks on SIP-Based VoIP Systems. In *Proceedings of the USENIX Workshop on Offensive Technologies (WOOT)*, 2007.

201. Y. Zhang and B. Singh. A Multi-Layer IPsec Protocol. In *Proceedings of the USENIX Security Symposium*, 2000.

202. P. Zimmermann, A. Johnston, and J. Callas. ZRTP: Media Path Key Agreement for Secure RTP. `http://zfoneproject.com/docs/ietf/draft-zimmermann-avt-zrtp-04.html`, 2007.

Index

μ-law, 43, 138, 143
1xEVDO, 25
700 MHz Spectrum, 42

A-law, 43
active attack, 11
AES, 14, 146
AGCH, 68
alarm, 20
AMPS, 24, 144
ASN.1, 59
attack signature, 21
AuC, 27
authentication, 10
authorization, 10

Base-Rate Fallacy, 22
BCH, 68
block cipher, 13, 150
Blue Box, 58
BSS, 29–30
BSSAP+, 111
BTS, 29

Call setup, 47
call-gapping, 159
Cap'n Crunch Whistle, 58
Carrier, 37
CCH, 68
CCS, 34
CDMA, 24, 39
Cellular Data
    history, 110–111
certificate authority, 16

cipher, 13
co-channel interference, 40
Community of Interest, 149
COMP128, 144
countermeasure, 11
credential, 15
credentials, 10
cryptography, 12
CSCF, 140
CSD, 110
customer, 2

Denial of service, 11, 76–82, 109, 118,
    151
DES, 13
Device Registration, 46
device state, 113, 143
digital rights management, 12
digital signature, 15
DMZ, 19
DTX, 44

eavesdropping, 11, 60
EDGE, 81, 110
EGPRS, 110
EGSM, 40
EIR, 27
End-to-End Argument, 128
ESME, 66
EV-DO, 143
EV-DV, 143

FDMA, 24, 37
firewall, 19

frequency hopping, 42

GGSN, 111
Go-Back-N, 35
GPRS, 24
  attack mitigation, 129–130
  attacking connection setup, 121–124
  attacking connection teardown,
      117–120
  blackbox testing, 116–117
  network elements, 30
  network elemments, 33
  packet multiplexing, 115–116
  registration, 111–112
  routeing packets, 112–115
  submitting packets, 112
GSM, 24
GSM-1800, 40
GSM-1900, 40
GSM-850, 40
GSM-900, 40
GTP, 112

H.323, 134–135
hash function, 14
HLR, 27–28, 111
HSCSD, 110
HSN, 42
HSS, 140

IAM, 47
IKE, 17
IMEI, 27
IMSI, 27
intrusion detection, 20
IP Multimedia Subsystem
    architecture, 140–141
IPsec, 17, 147
ISDN, 36

jamming, 61

Kirkoff's principal, 13

Location Area, 29

malware, 63
man in the middle, 148
MAPsec, 48–49
MCEF, 70

message authentication code, 15
micro-cell, 41
MSC, 29, 32
MSRN, 47
MTP, 34
multipath distortion, 38, 42
mutip-factor authentication, 15

National Communications System, 79
network design conflict, 124–129
network intrusion detection systems, 20
NIST, 152
NSA, 152
NSP, 36

open functionality, 11
overload, 62

P-TMSI, 113
PACCH, 114
PAGCH, 114
passive attacks, 11
PBCCH, 116
PCH, 68, 77
PCM, 43, 150
PDCH, 115
PDP, 111
PDTCH, 123
pico-cell, 41
PKI, 145
PM, 49
port scanning, 21
PPCH, 114
PRACH, 114, 119
principals, 10
privacy, 62
provider, 2
public key cryptogrphy, 14

Quad-band Phone, 40
Quality of Service, 31
Queue Management
  blackbox testing, 70–71
  weighted fair queuing, 89–92
  weighted random early detection,
      92–96

RACH, 68, 77, 119
Reconnaissance

Additional Methods, 75–76
NPA/NXX, 73
Provider Webpages, 74–75
Web Scraping, 73–74
Resource Management
direct channel allocation, 102–105
dynamic resource provisioning,
100–102
strict resource provisioning, 97–100
Routing Area, 33
RPT-LTE, 43
RSA, 14
RTCP, 139
RTP, 138, 139

SCCP, 35
SCP, 34
SDCCH, 68, 77
secret key algorithm, 13
security association, 17
security association datasbase, 17
SGSN, 111
shared key algorithm, 13
Short Messaging Service
attacks on cities, 77–81
attacks on individuals, 76–77
attacks on regions, 81–82
bottlenecks, 69–72
characterizing attacks on, 85–86
current solutions, 87–89
delivery of, 66–69
history of, 66
injecting messages, 71–72
network, 82–84
over GPRS, 81
SID, 45
SIM, 27
SIP
history of, 134–135
in IMS, 140
making calls, 139–140
messages, 136–138
proxy, 135–136
registrar, 135
SIPS, 145, 148
SMPP, 71

SMSC, 66–67
SRTCP, 146
SRTP, 146
SS7
Network, 33–34
Protocols, 34–36
vulnerabilities, 58
SSL, 18
STP, 34
stream cipher, 13, 146, 150

TACS, 24, 38
TBF, 116
TCH, 68, 77, 120
TDMA, 24, 38
TFI, 116, 118, 125
threat model, 152
TLS, 18, 145
TMSI, 68, 77
traffic analysis, 149
transit security, 10
transport security, 10
Tri-band Phone, 40
trust, 11
trust model, 12

UMTS, 25
URI, 140

VAD, 44
virutal private network, 18
VLR, 29
VOIP, 11
VoIP, 2
vulnerabilities, 11

WCDMA, 25
Weak Cryptography
A3/A8, 49, 55
A5, 49, 56
COMP128, 50, 55
WiMax, 143

X.25, 31

ZRTP, 147